—— IN THE NAME OF ALLAH ——

This book contains the 99 names of Allah
which are considered to be
the attributes of Allah

Learning and memorizing the names of Allah
will help us to better know him
and worship him

The Beautiful Names of Allah
Coloring and Activity
Book for Muslim

Translate name of Allah meaning

this book belong to

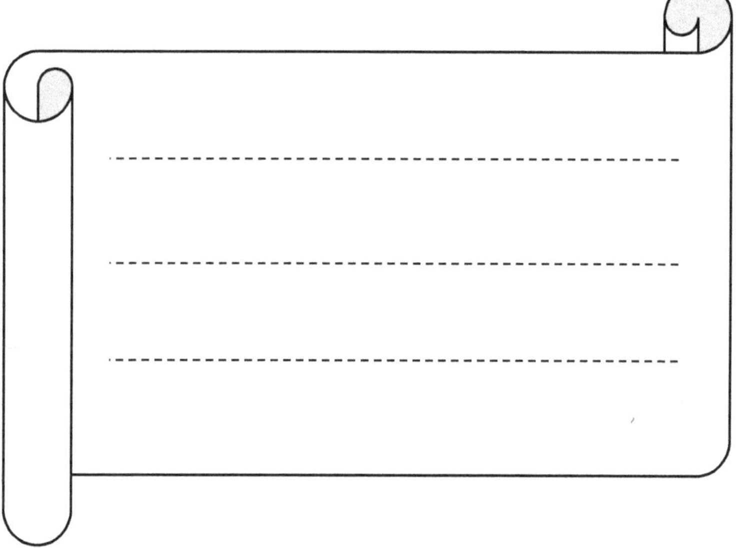

الله

Allah

The Greatest Name

الرحمن

Al Rahman

The All-Compassionate

الرحيم

Al Rahim

The All-Merciful

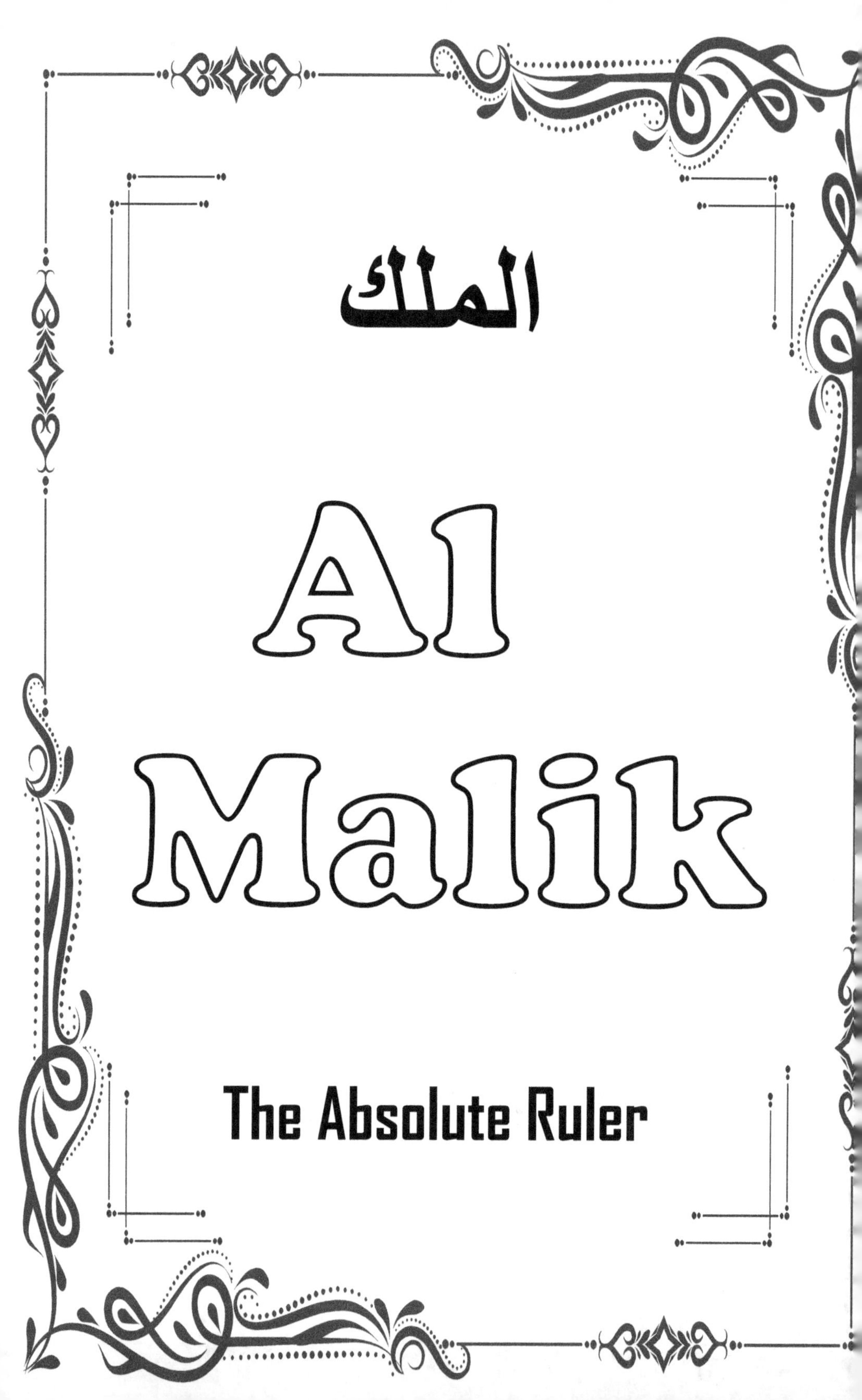

الملك

Al Malik

The Absolute Ruler

القدوس

Al Quddus

The Pure One

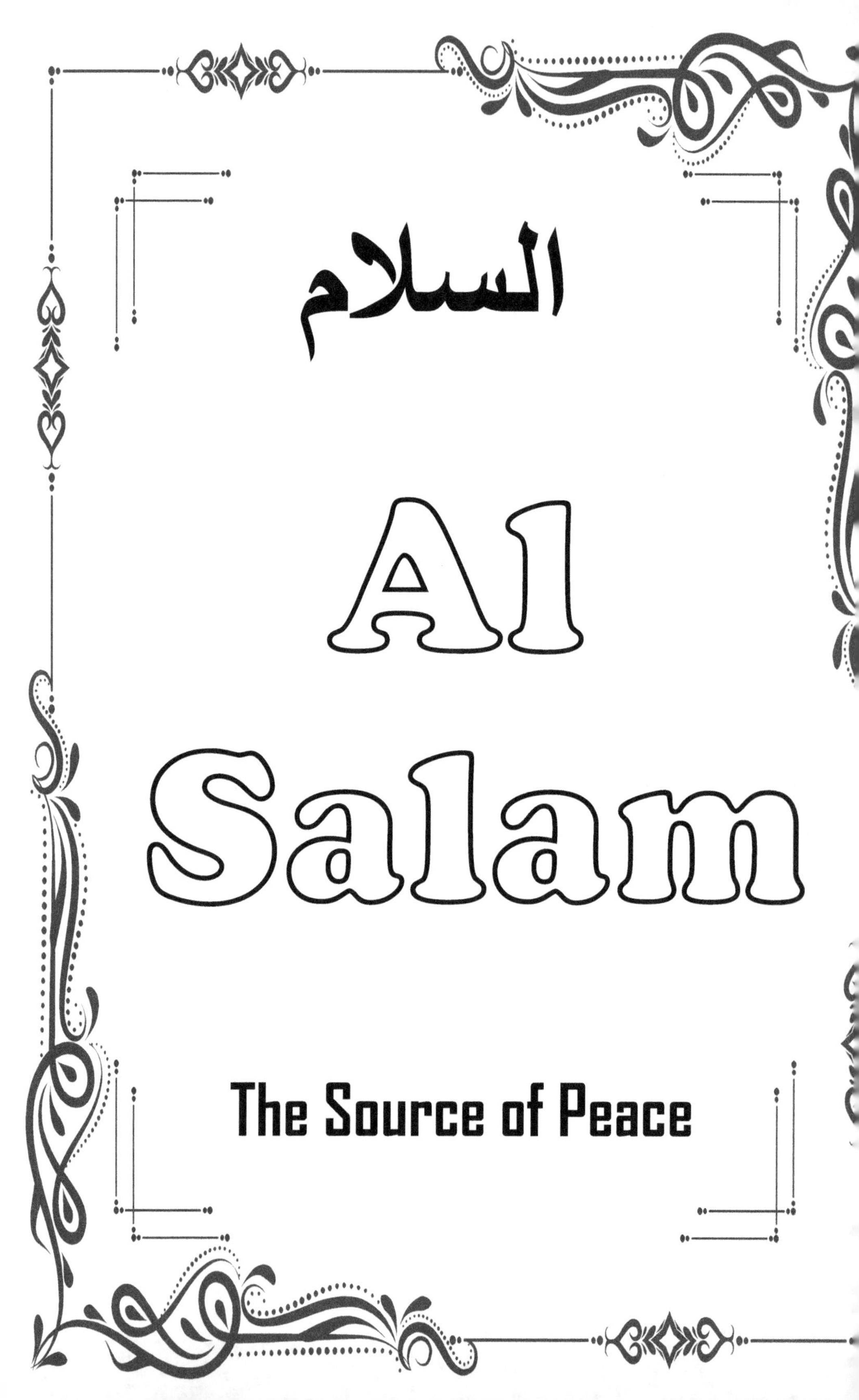
السلام

Al Salam

The Source of Peace

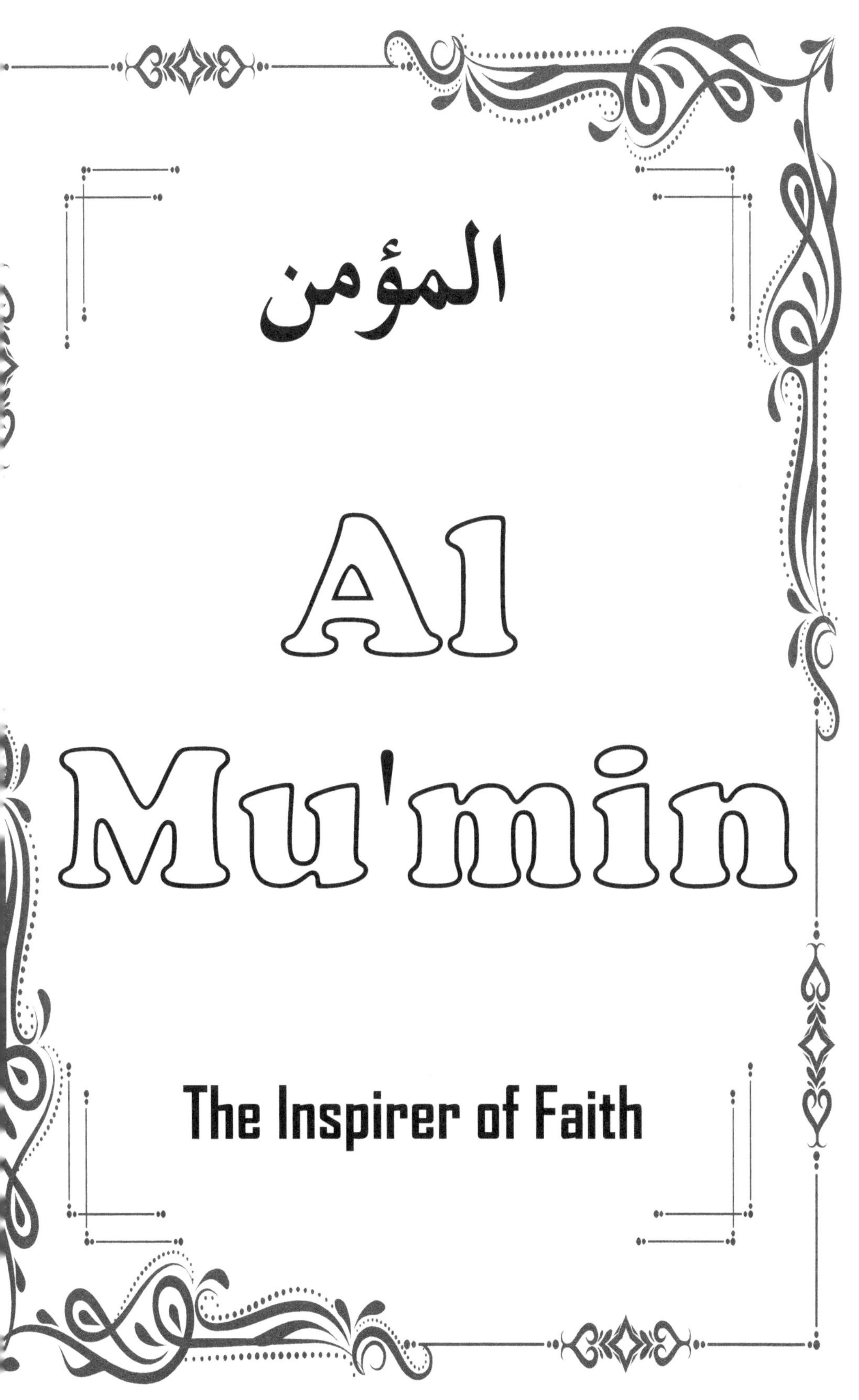

المؤمن

Al Mu'min

The Inspirer of Faith

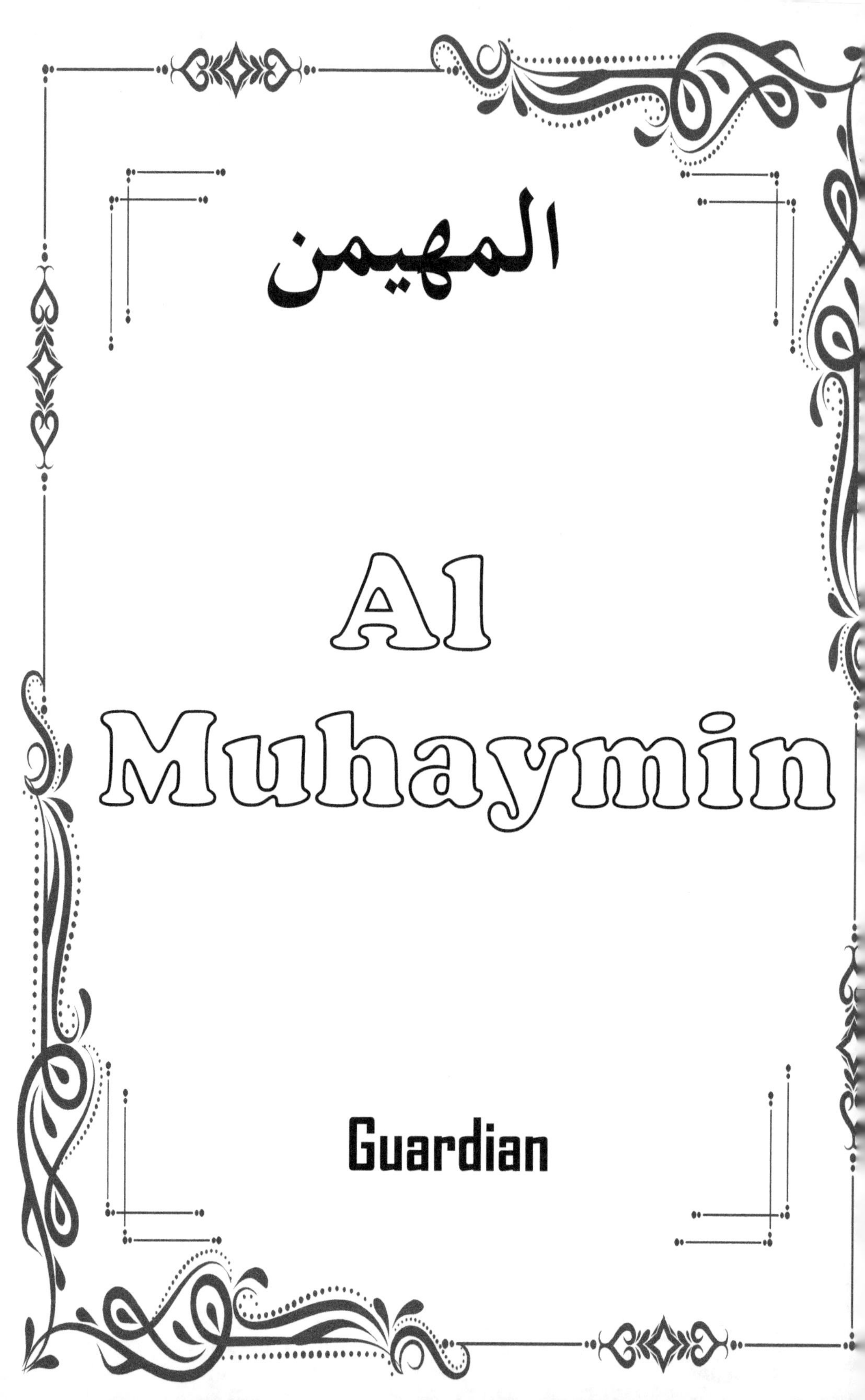
المهيمن

Al
Muhaymin

Guardian

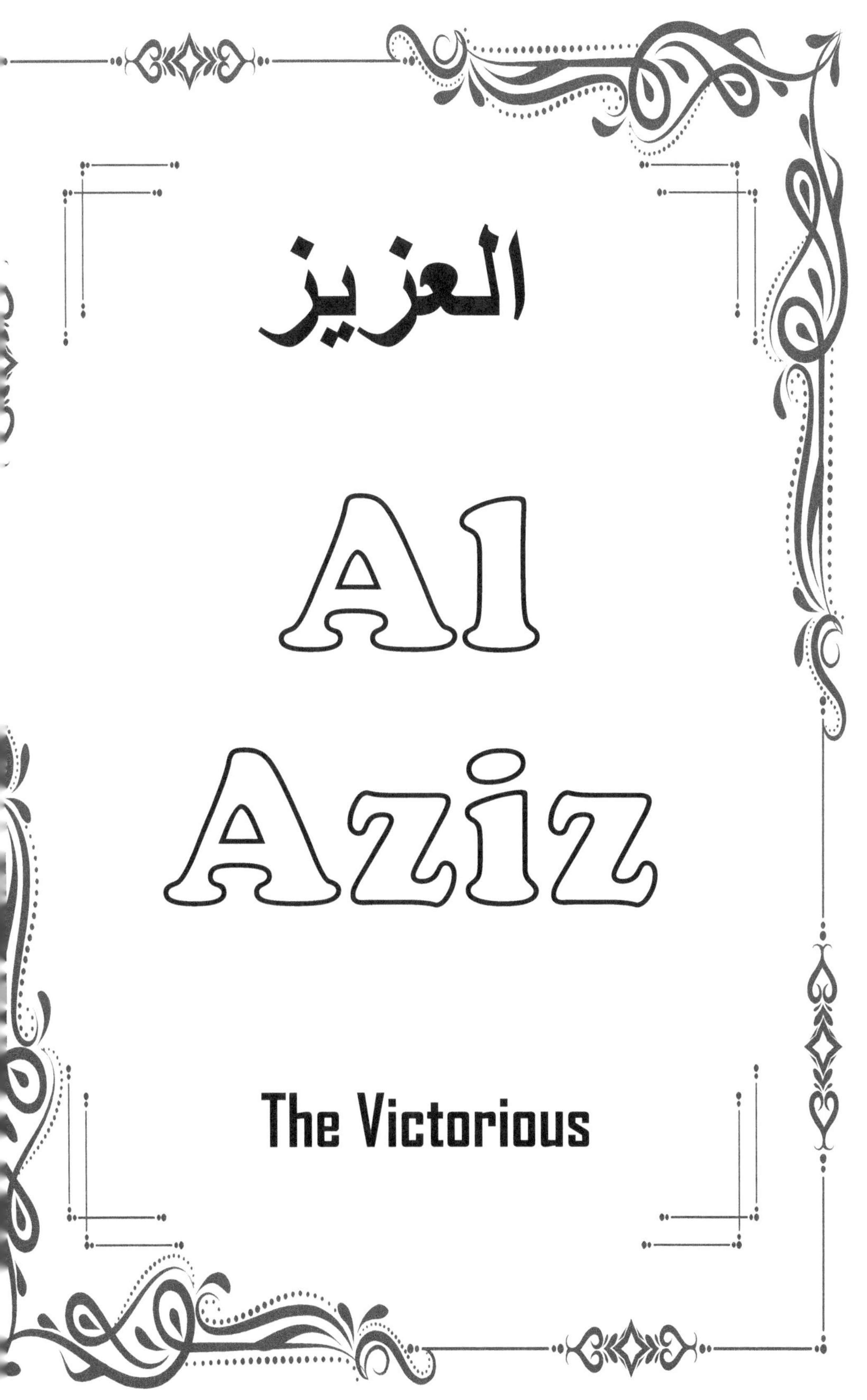

العزيز

Al Aziz

The Victorious

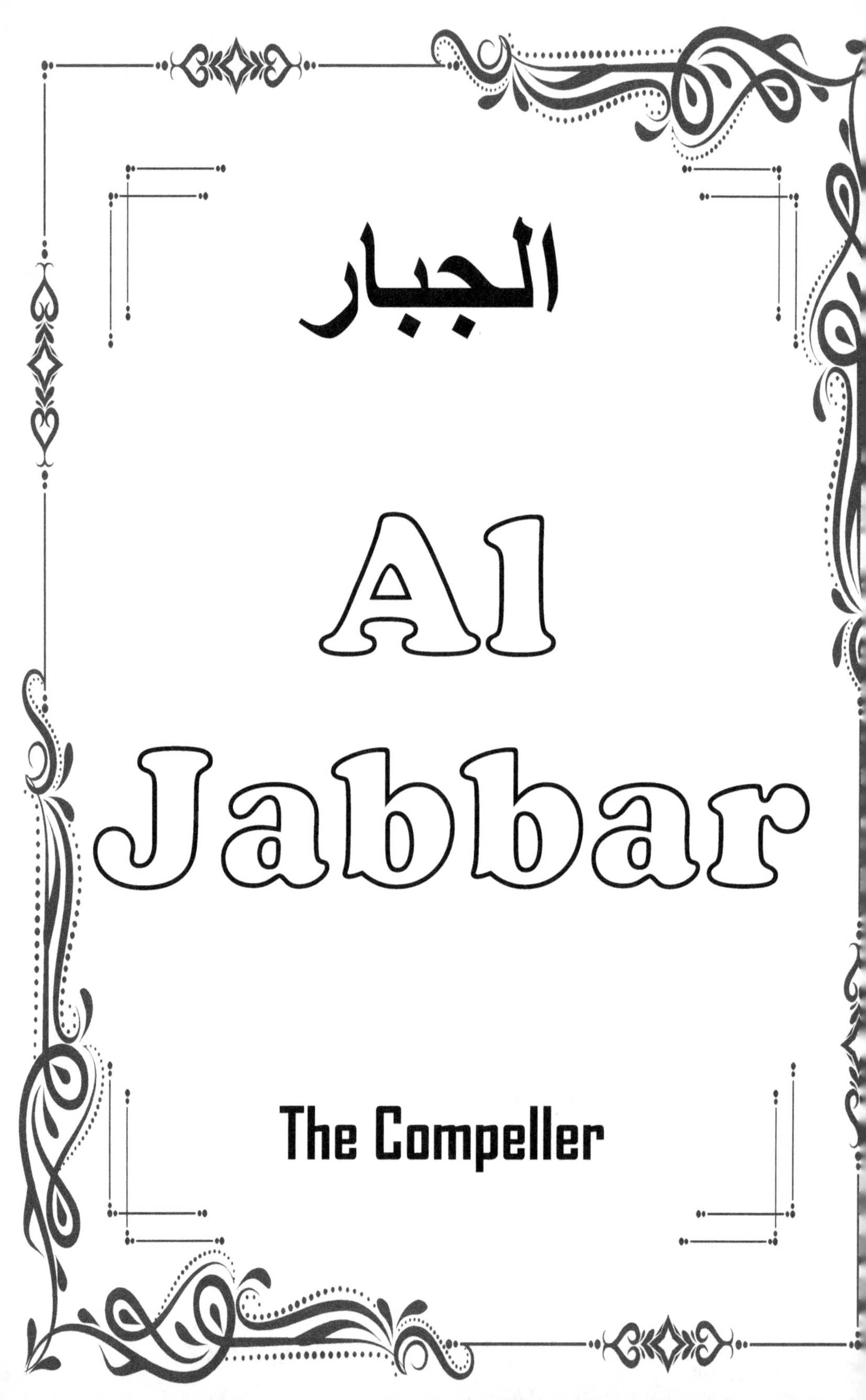

الجبار
Al Jabbar
The Compeller

المتكبر

Al Mutakabbir

The Greatest

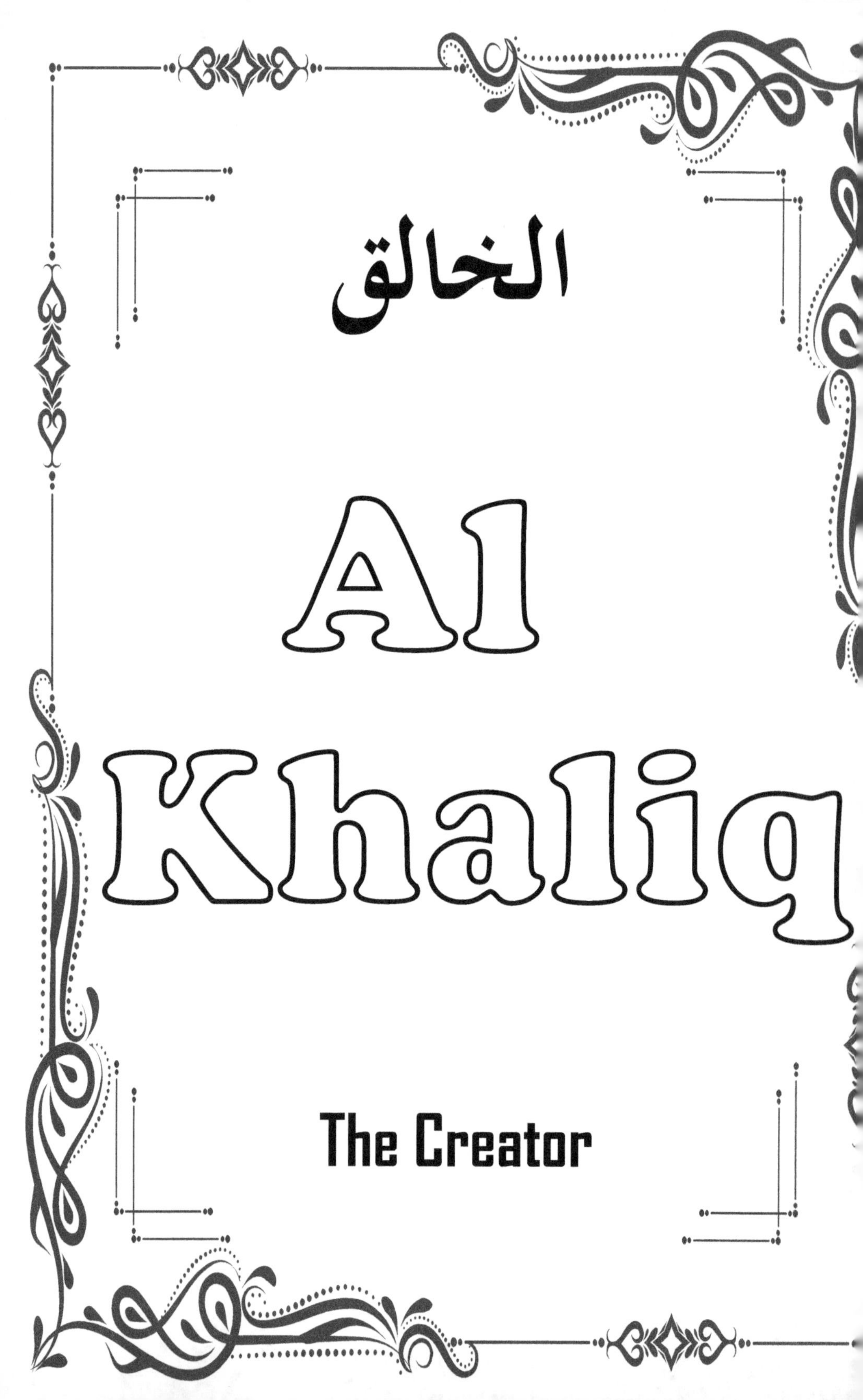

الخالق

Al Khaliq

The Creator

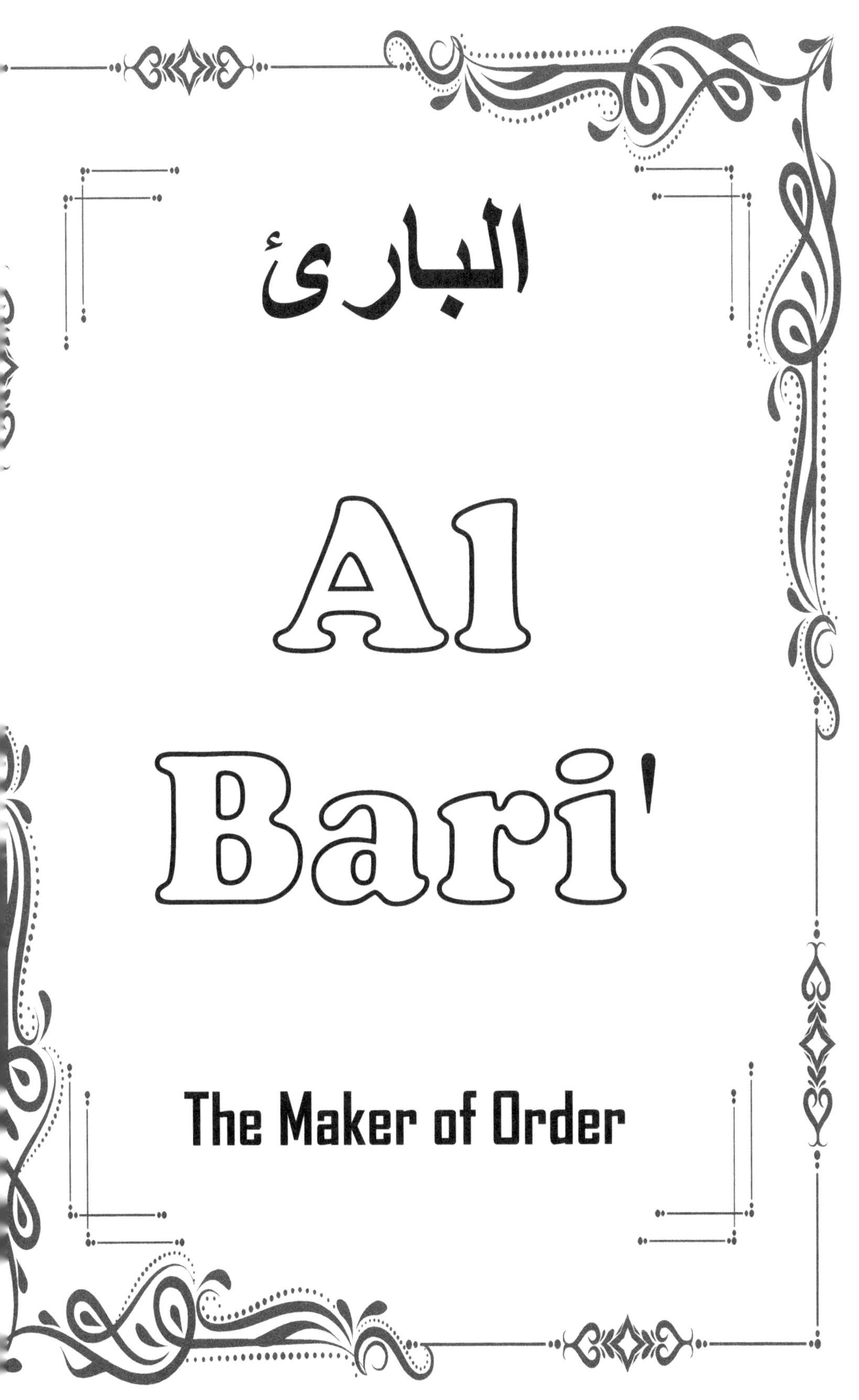# الباری

Al Bari'

The Maker of Order

المصور

Al
Musawwir

The Shaper of Beauty

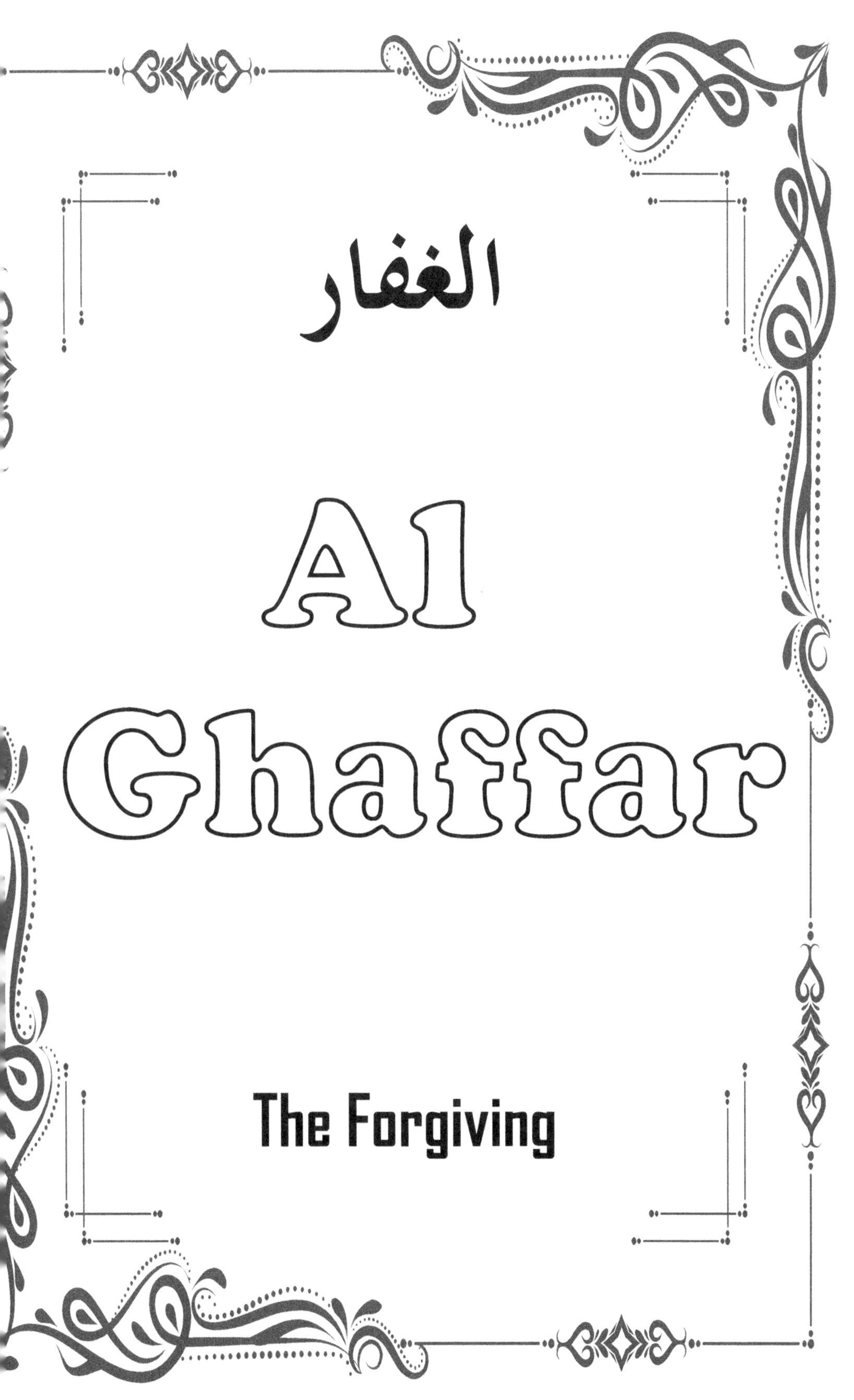
الغفار

Al Ghaffar

The Forgiving

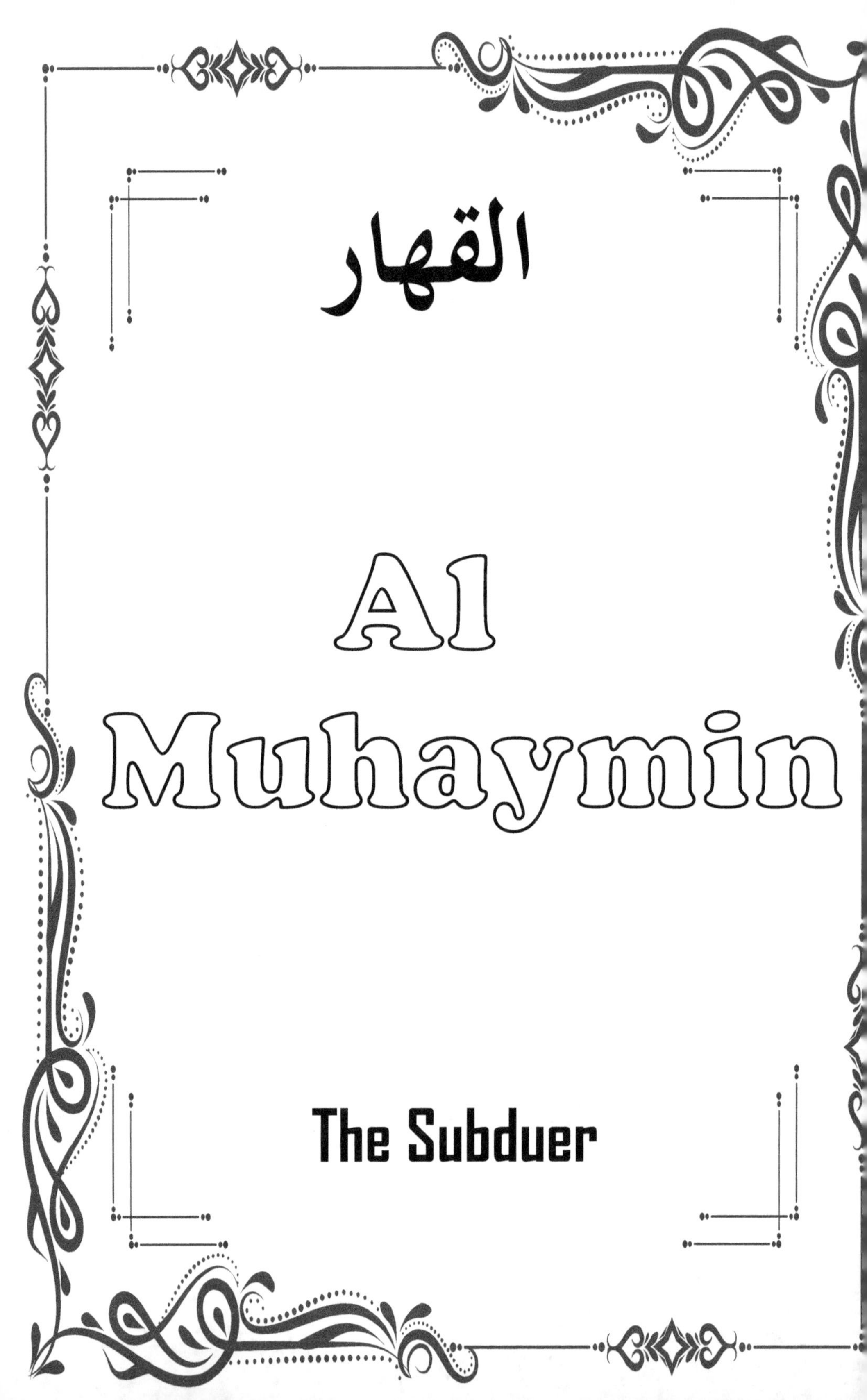
القهار

Al
Muhaymin

The Subduer

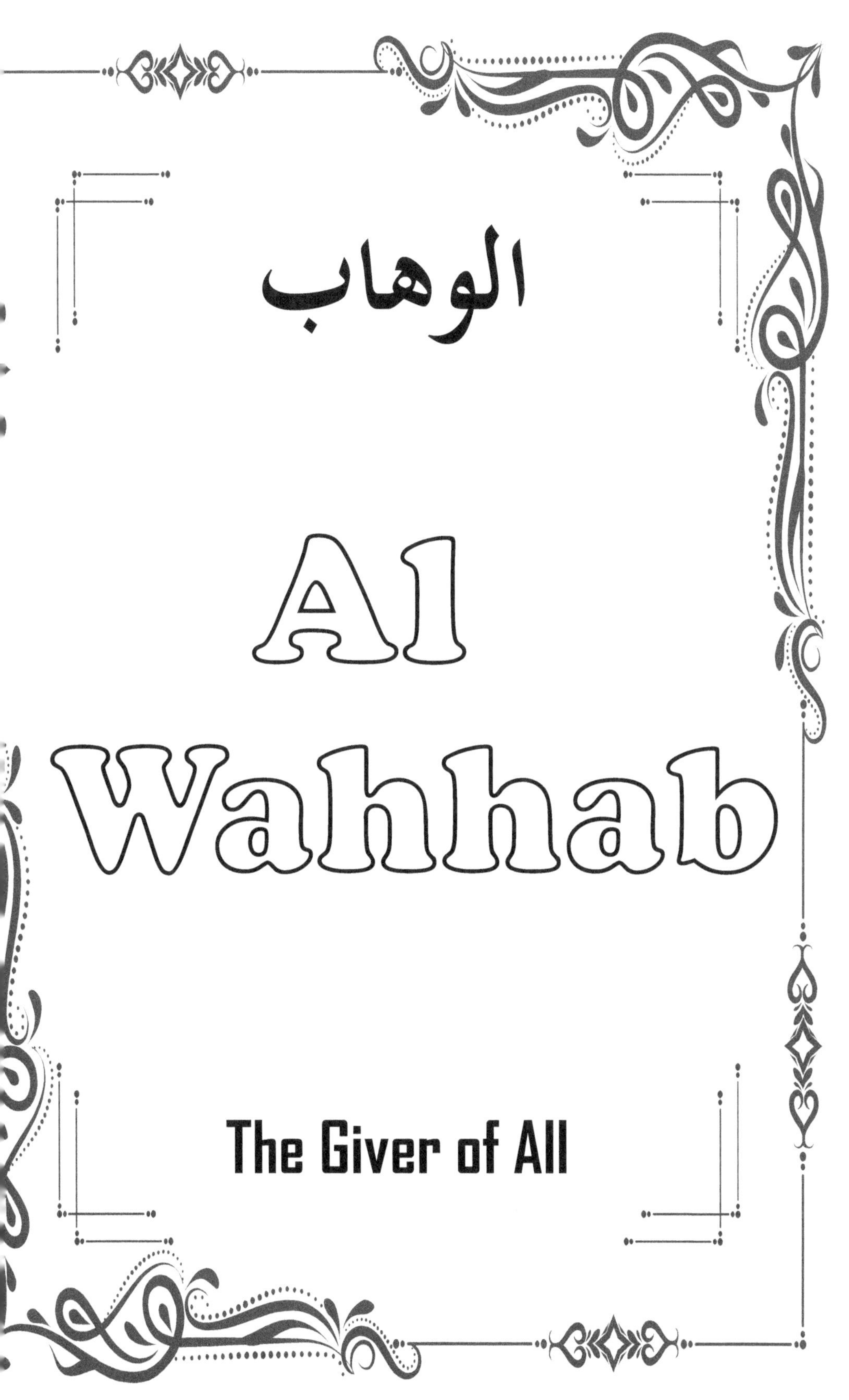
الوهاب

Al Wahhab

The Giver of All

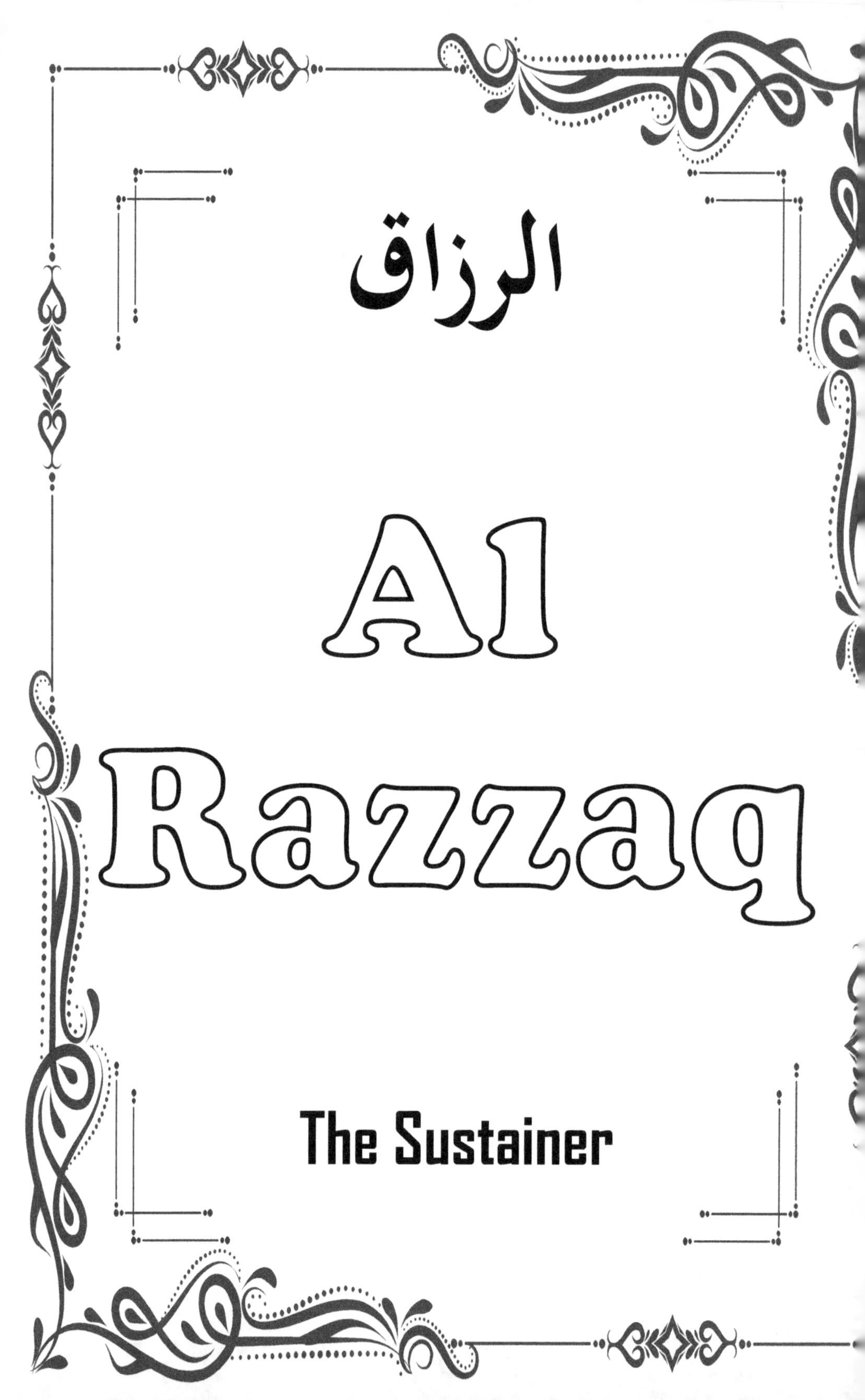

الرزاق
Al
Razzaq
The Sustainer

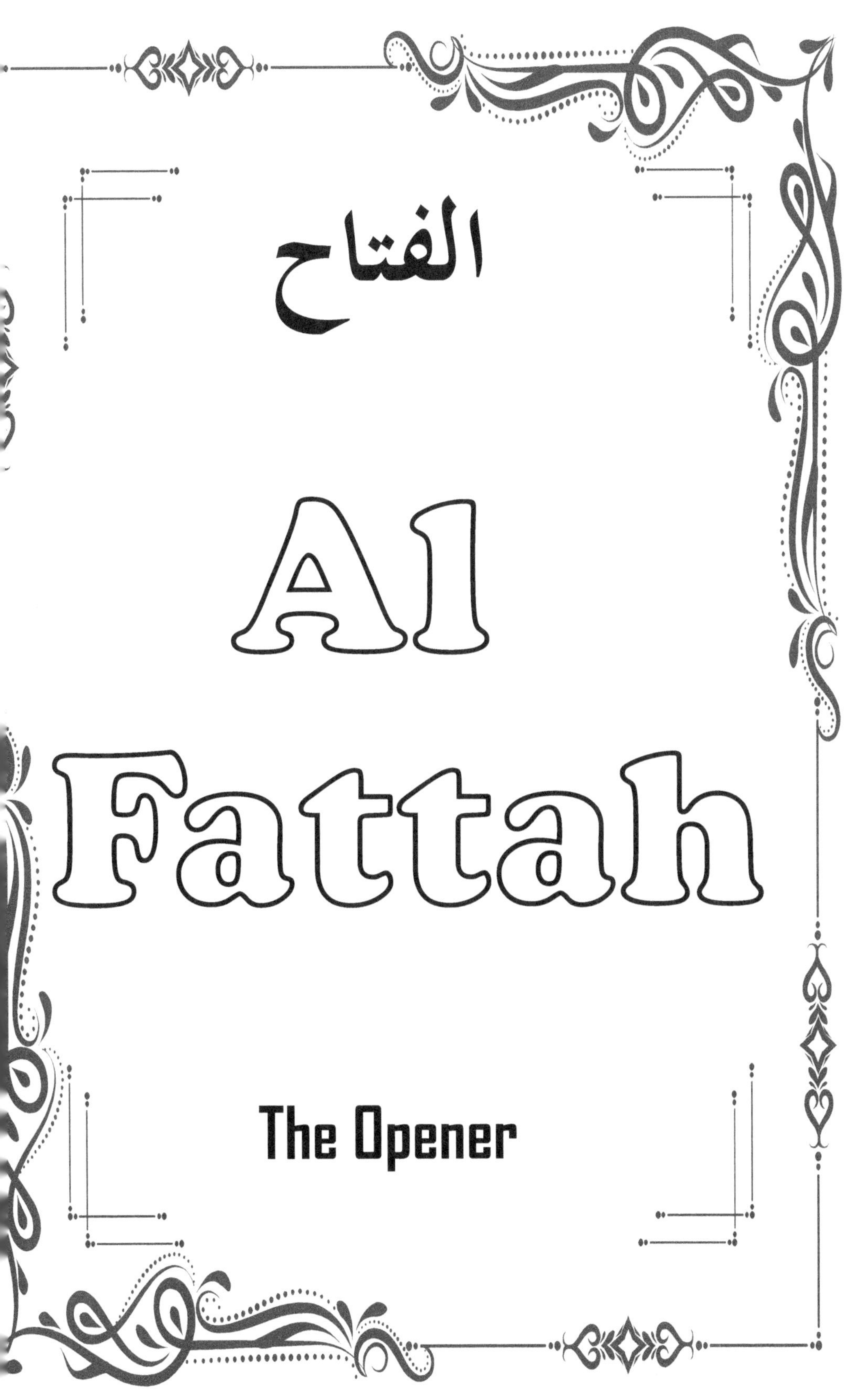

Al Fattah

The Opener

العليم

Al
Alim

The Knower of All

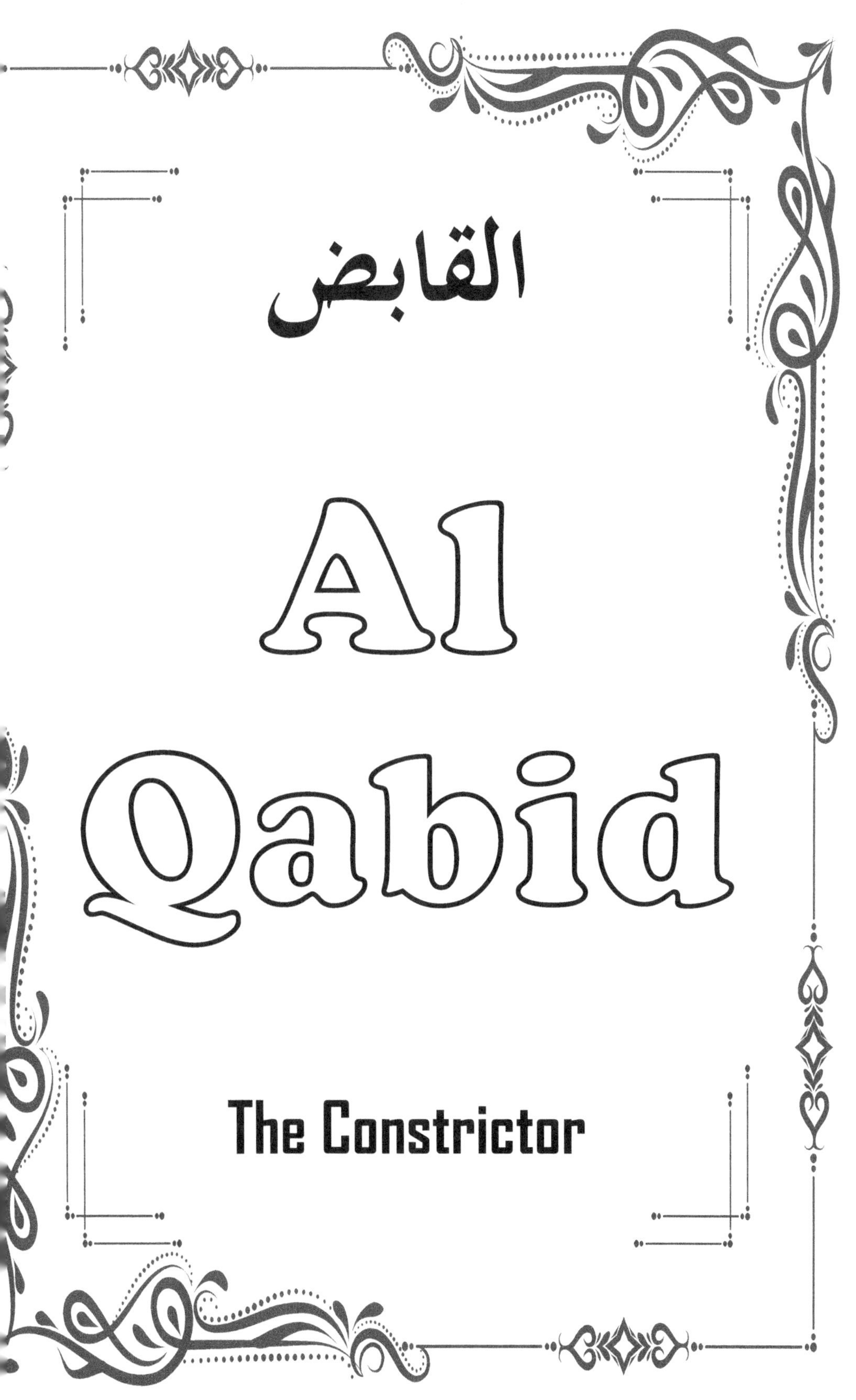

القابض

Al Qabid

The Constrictor

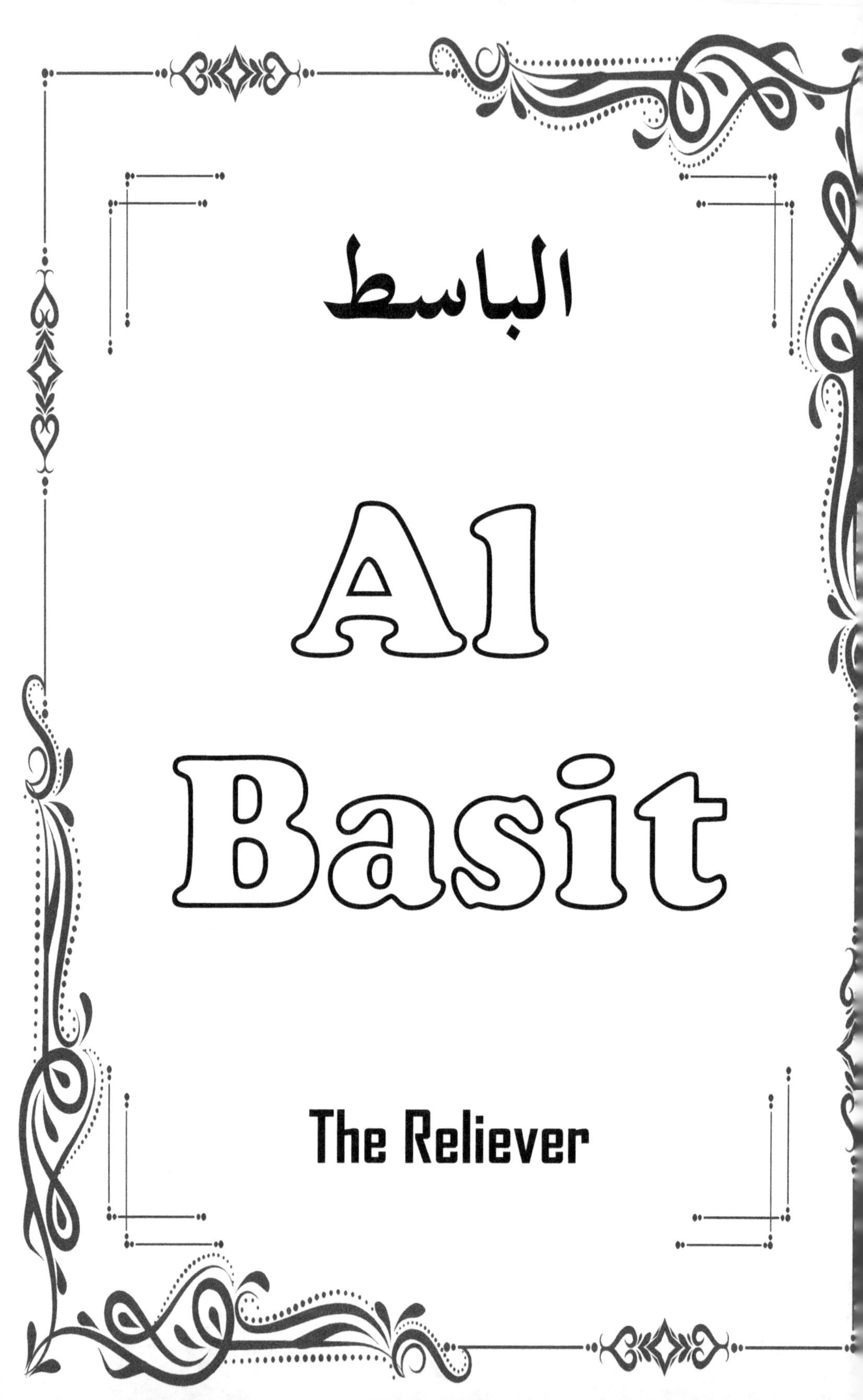

الباسط

Al
Basit

The Reliever

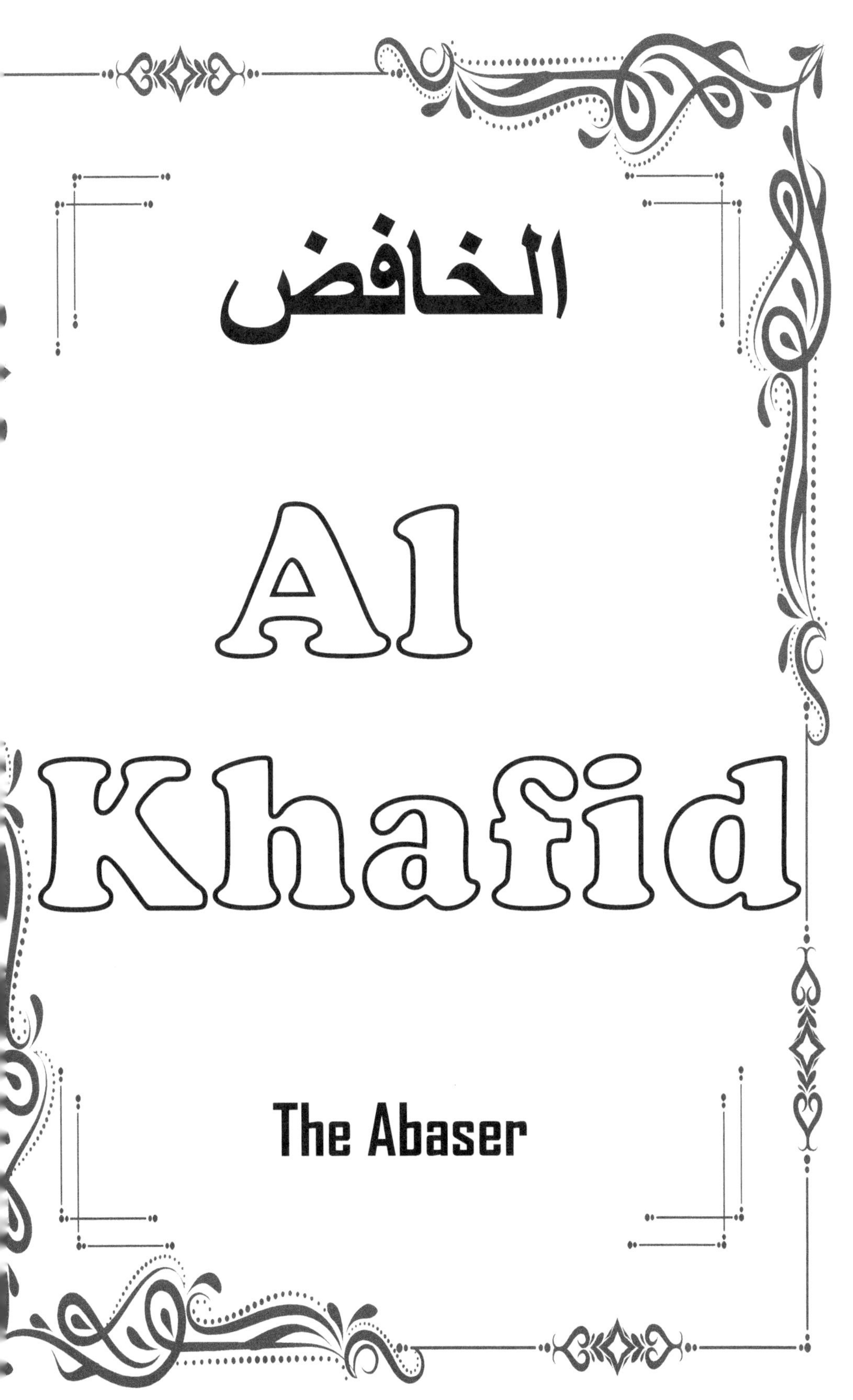

الخافض

Al Khafid

The Abaser

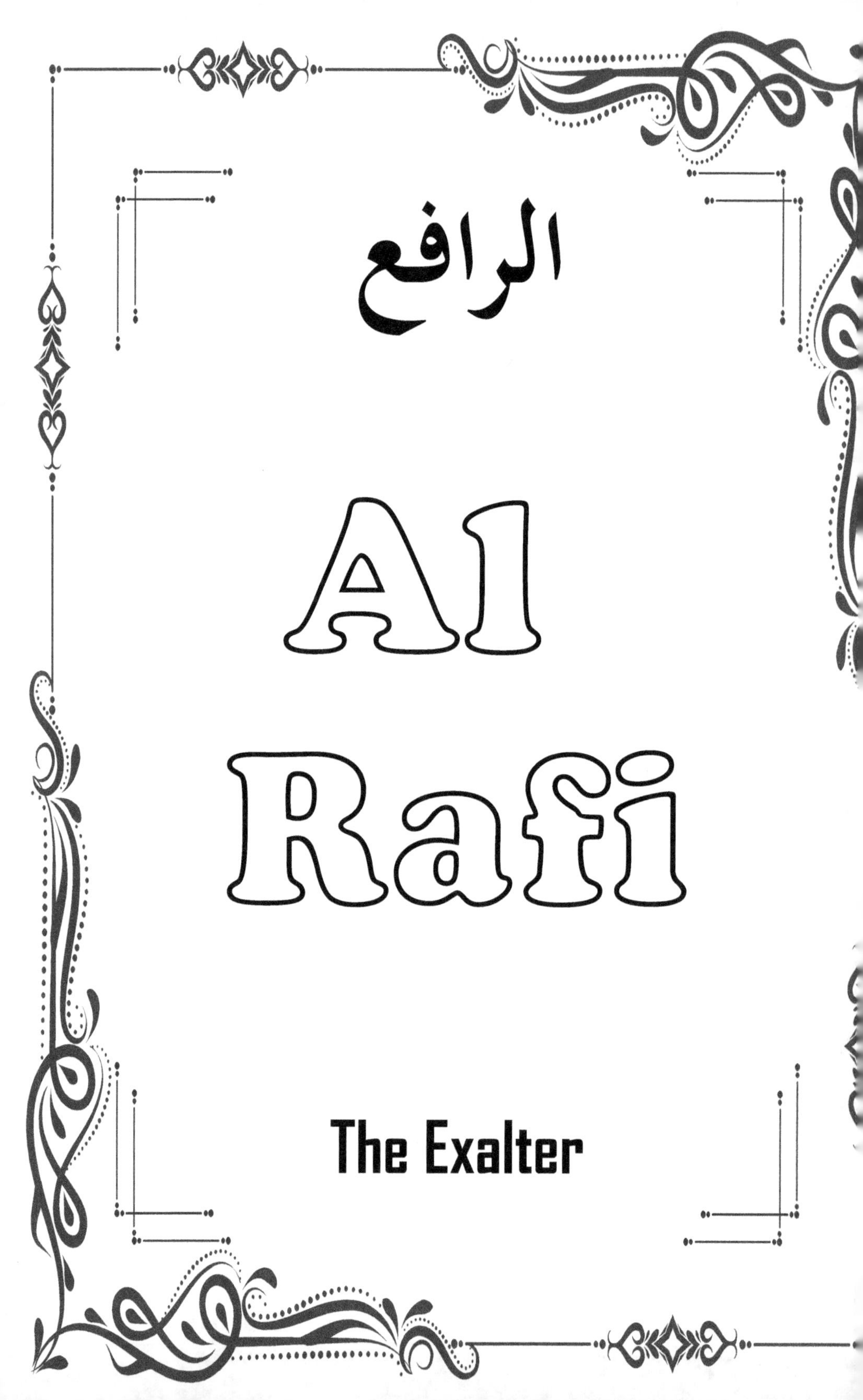

الرافع

Al
Rafi

The Exalter

المعز

Al Mu'izz

The Bestower of Honors

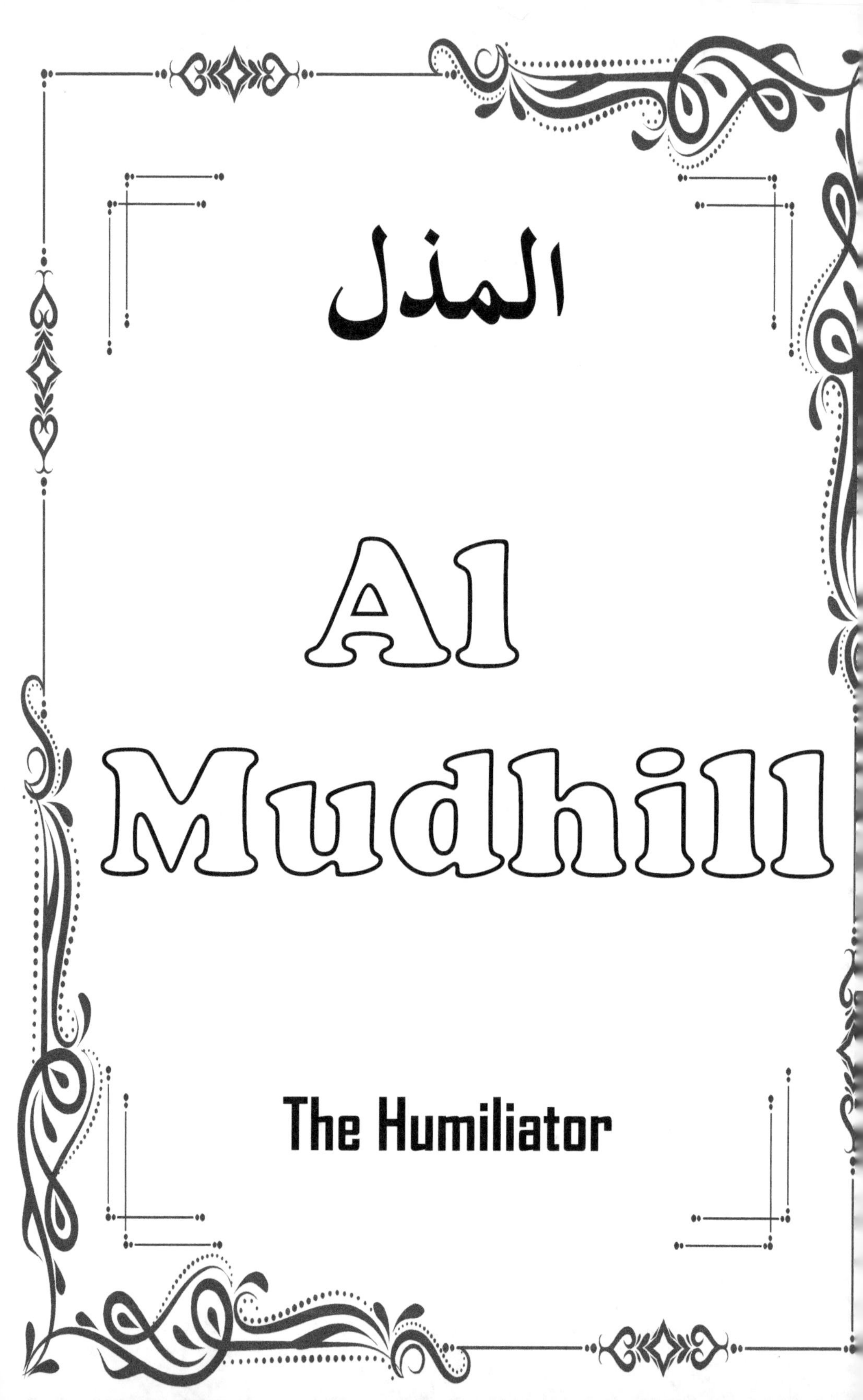

المذل

Al Mudhill

The Humiliator

السميع

Al Sami

The Hearer of All

البصير
Al
Basir
The Seer of All

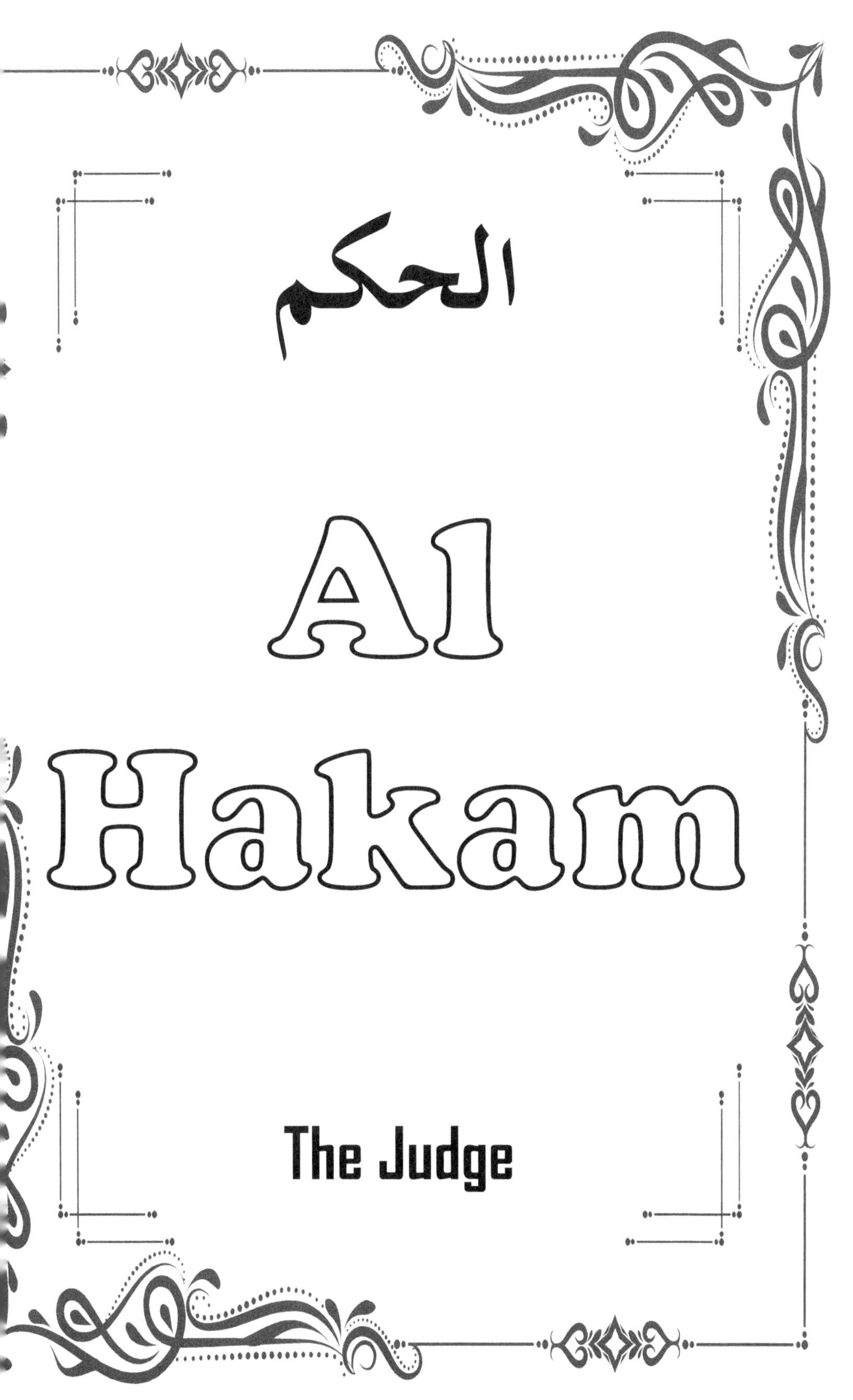

الحكم

Al Hakam

The Judge

العدل

Al
Adl

The Just

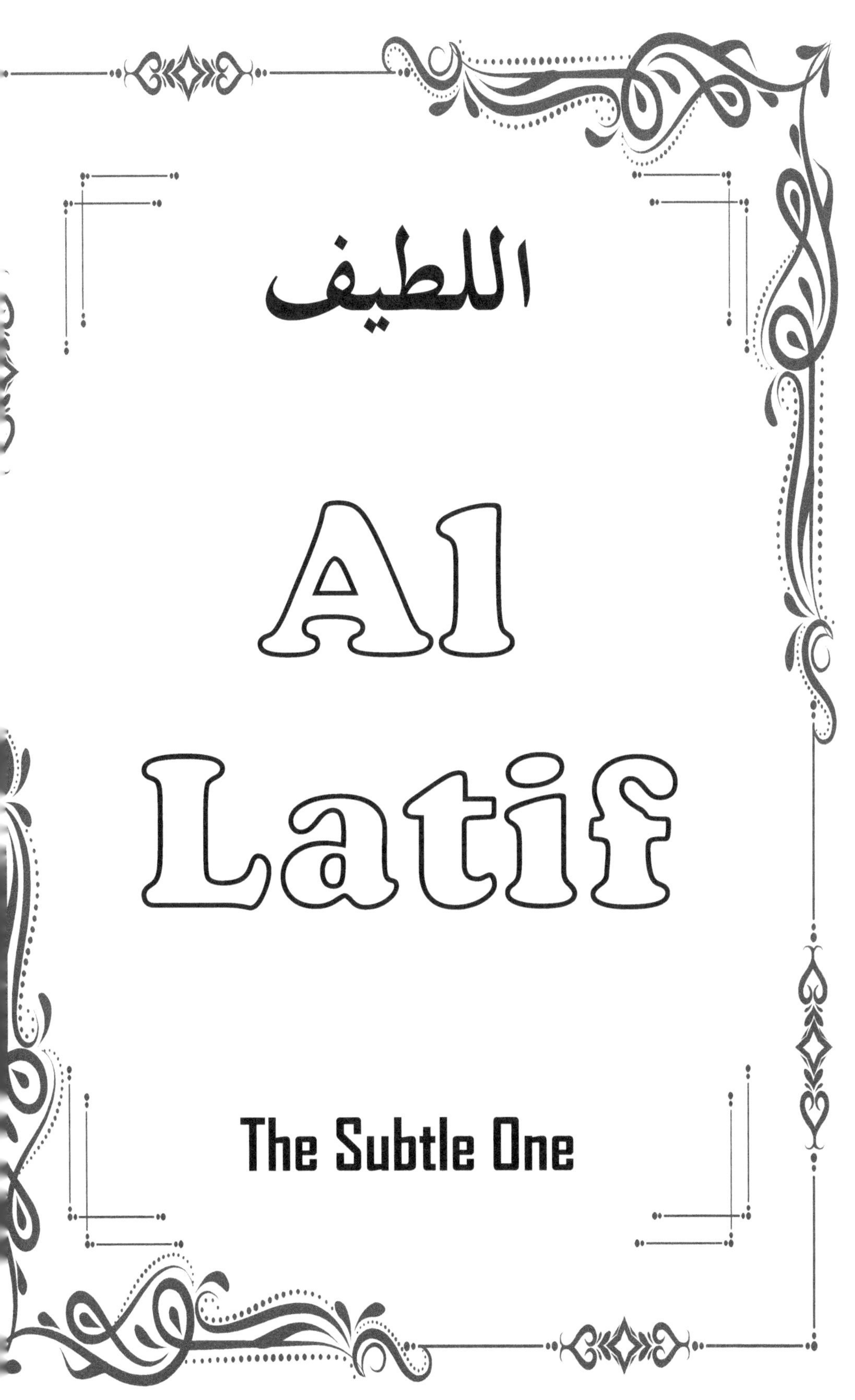
اللطيف

Al
Latif

The Subtle One

الخبير

Al
Khabir

The All-Aware

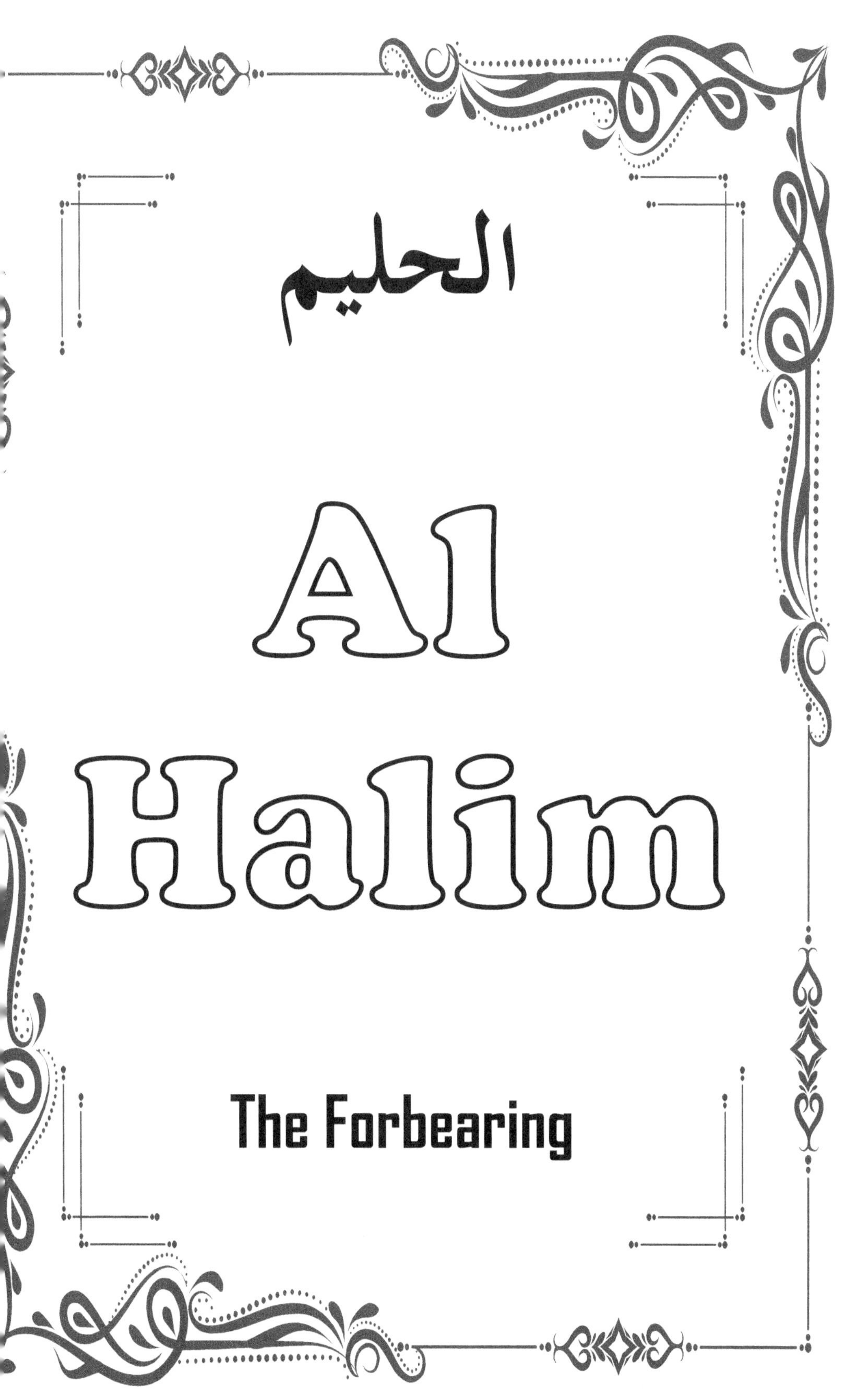

الحليم

Al

Halim

The Forbearing

العظيم

Al
Azim

The Magnificent

الغفور

Al Ghafur

The Forgiver and Hider of Faults

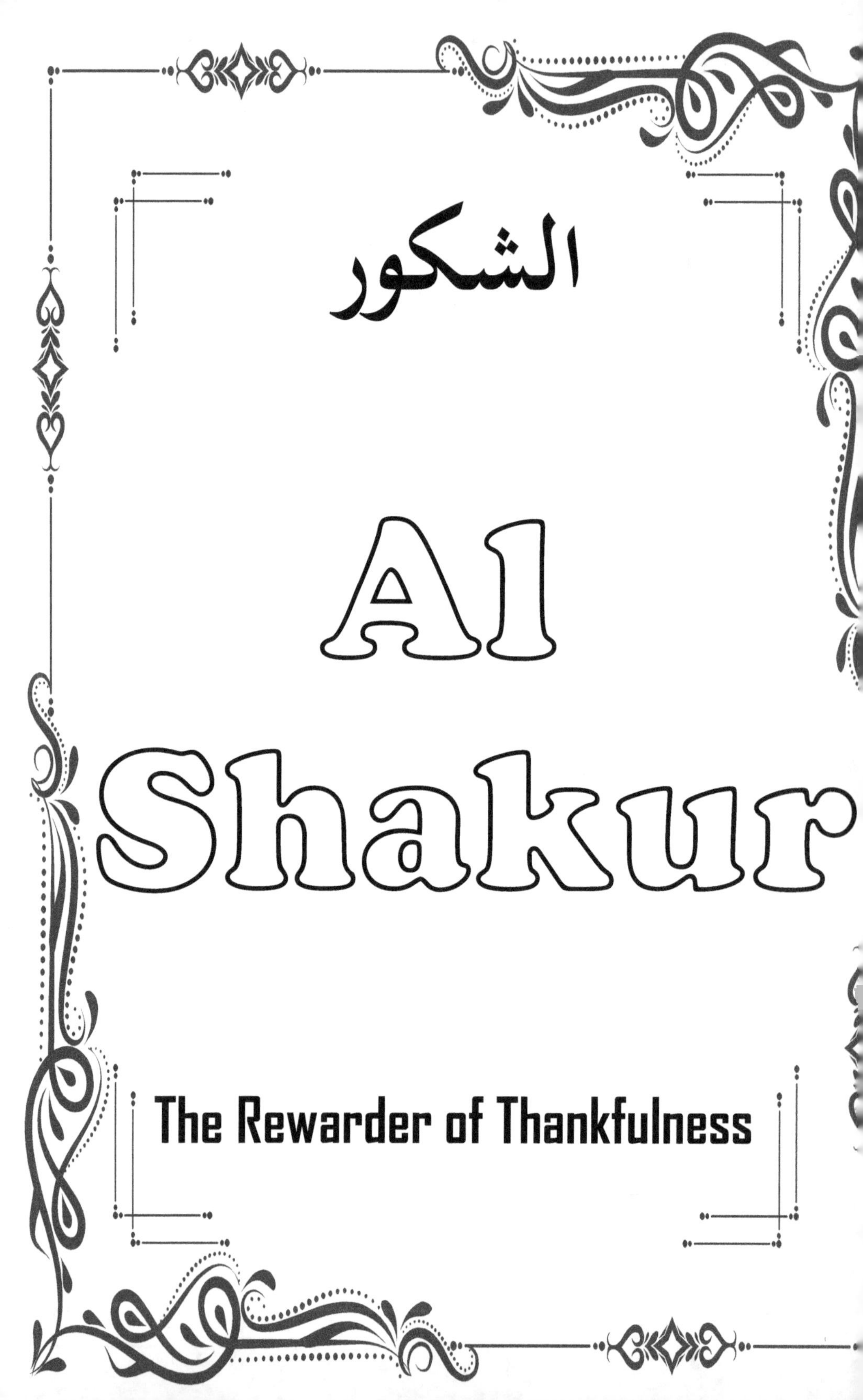الشكور

Al Shakur

The Rewarder of Thankfulness

العلي

Al
Ali

The Highest

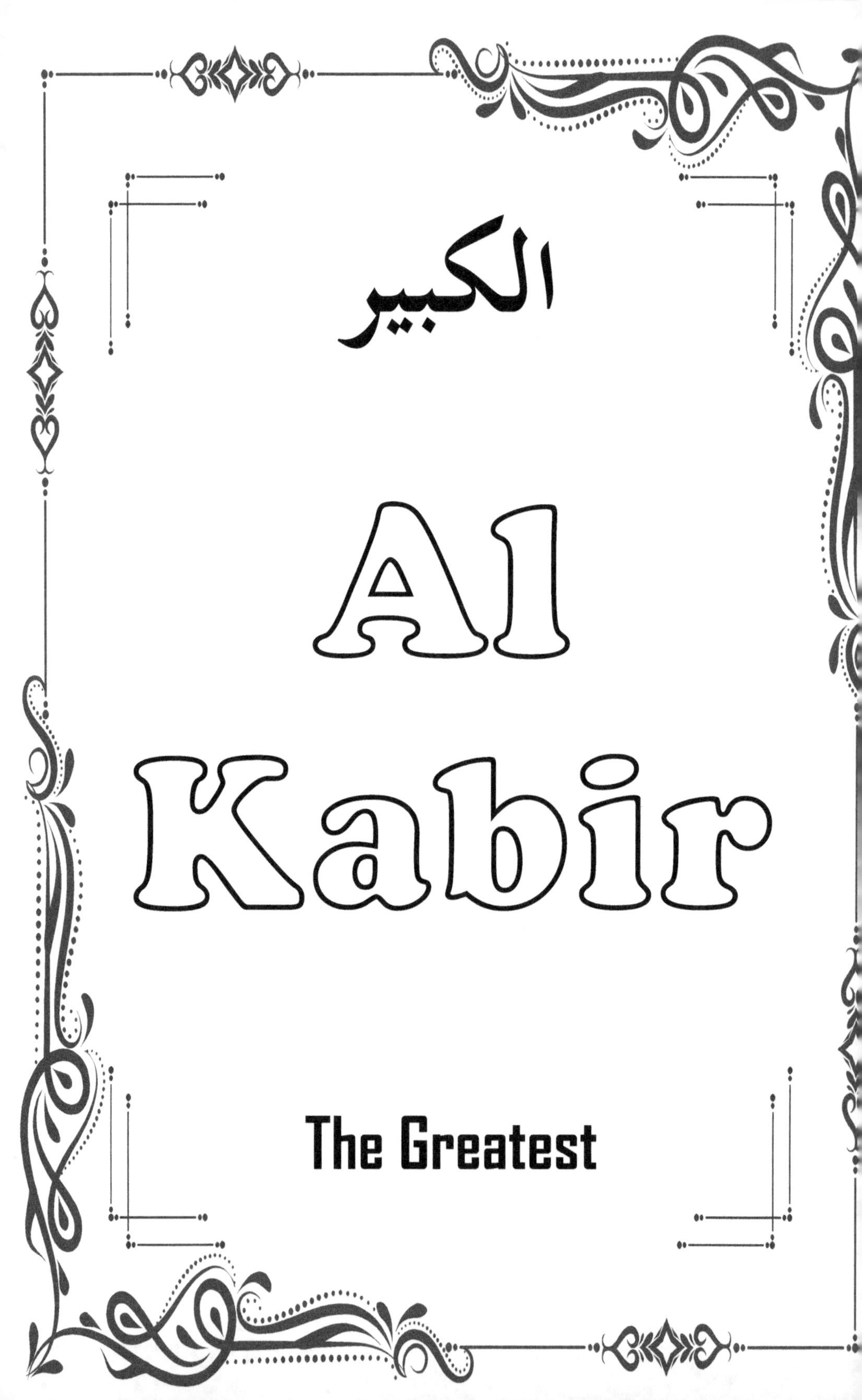

الكبير

Al Kabir

The Greatest

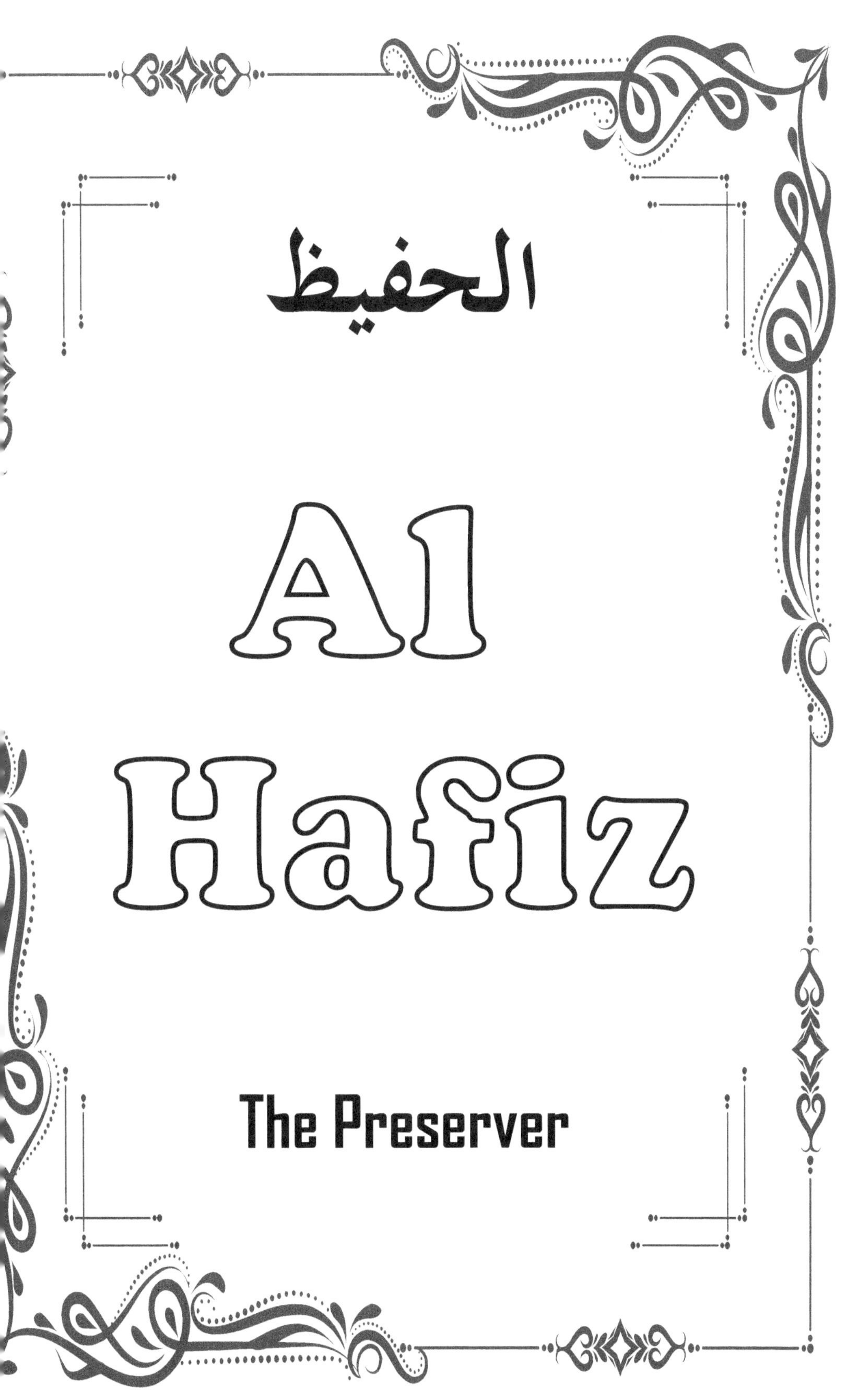

الحفيظ

Al
Hafiz

The Preserver

المقيت

Al Muqit

The Nourisher

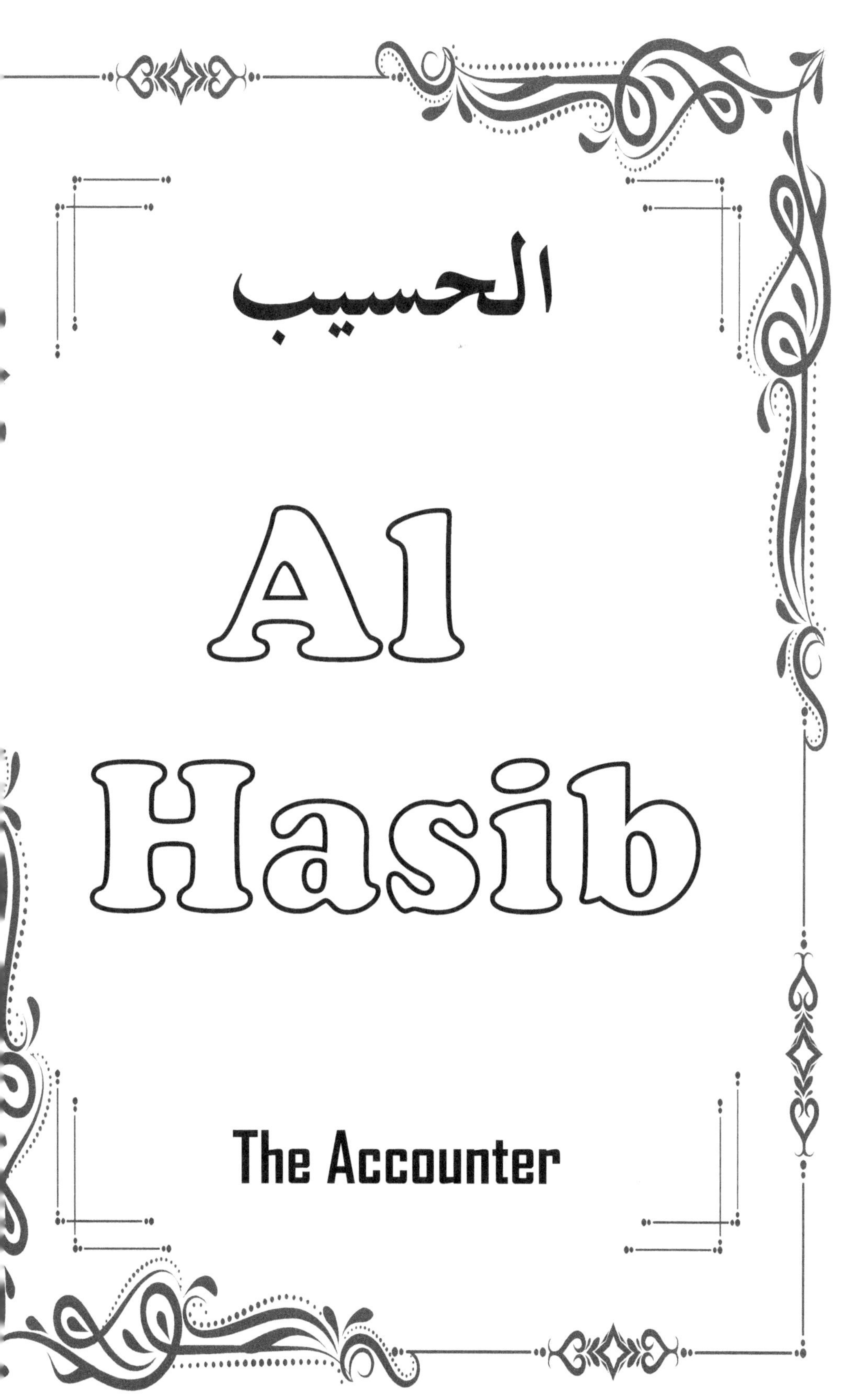

الحسيب
Al
Hasib
The Accounter

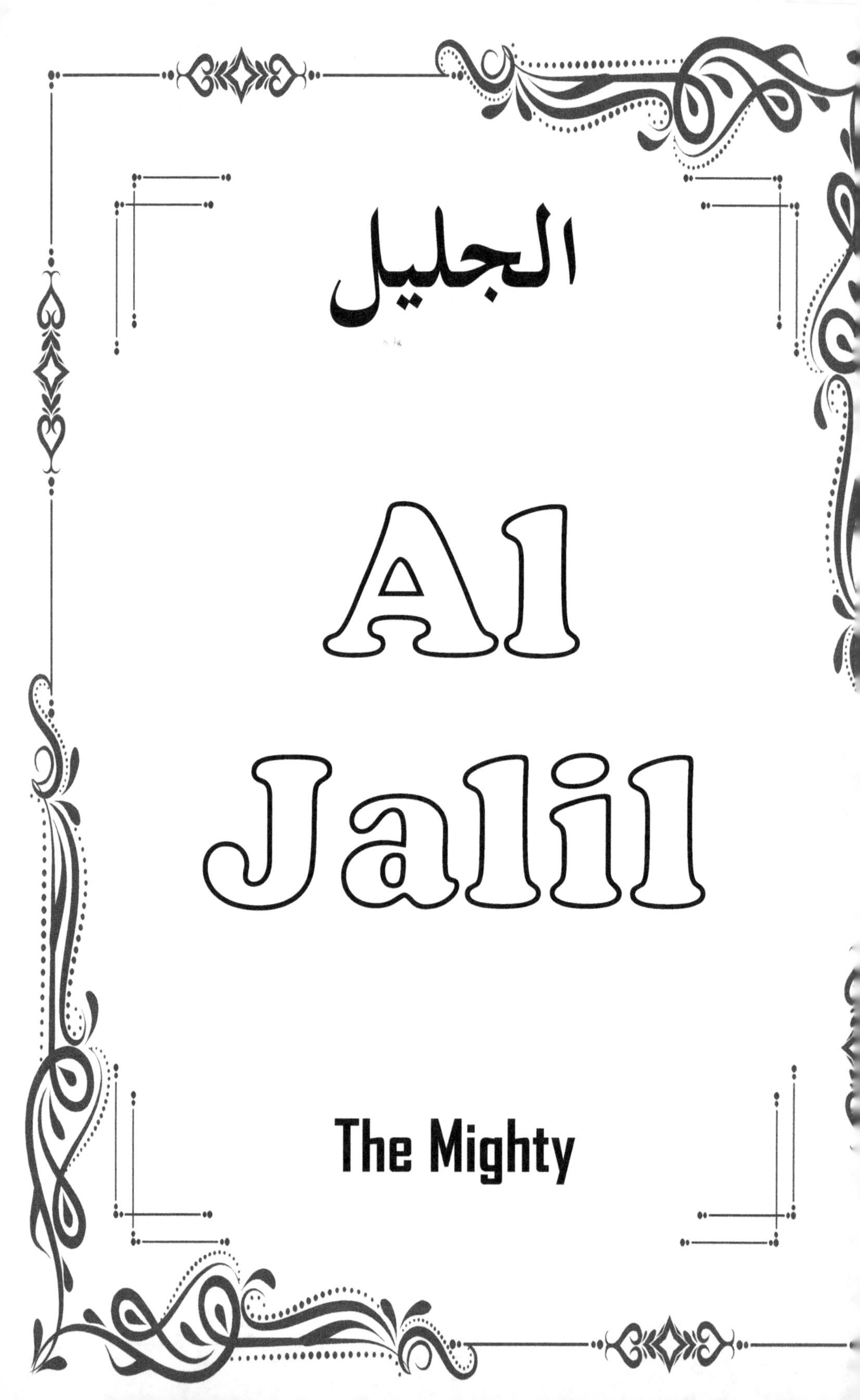

الجليل

Al
Jalil

The Mighty

الكريم

Al Karim

The Generous

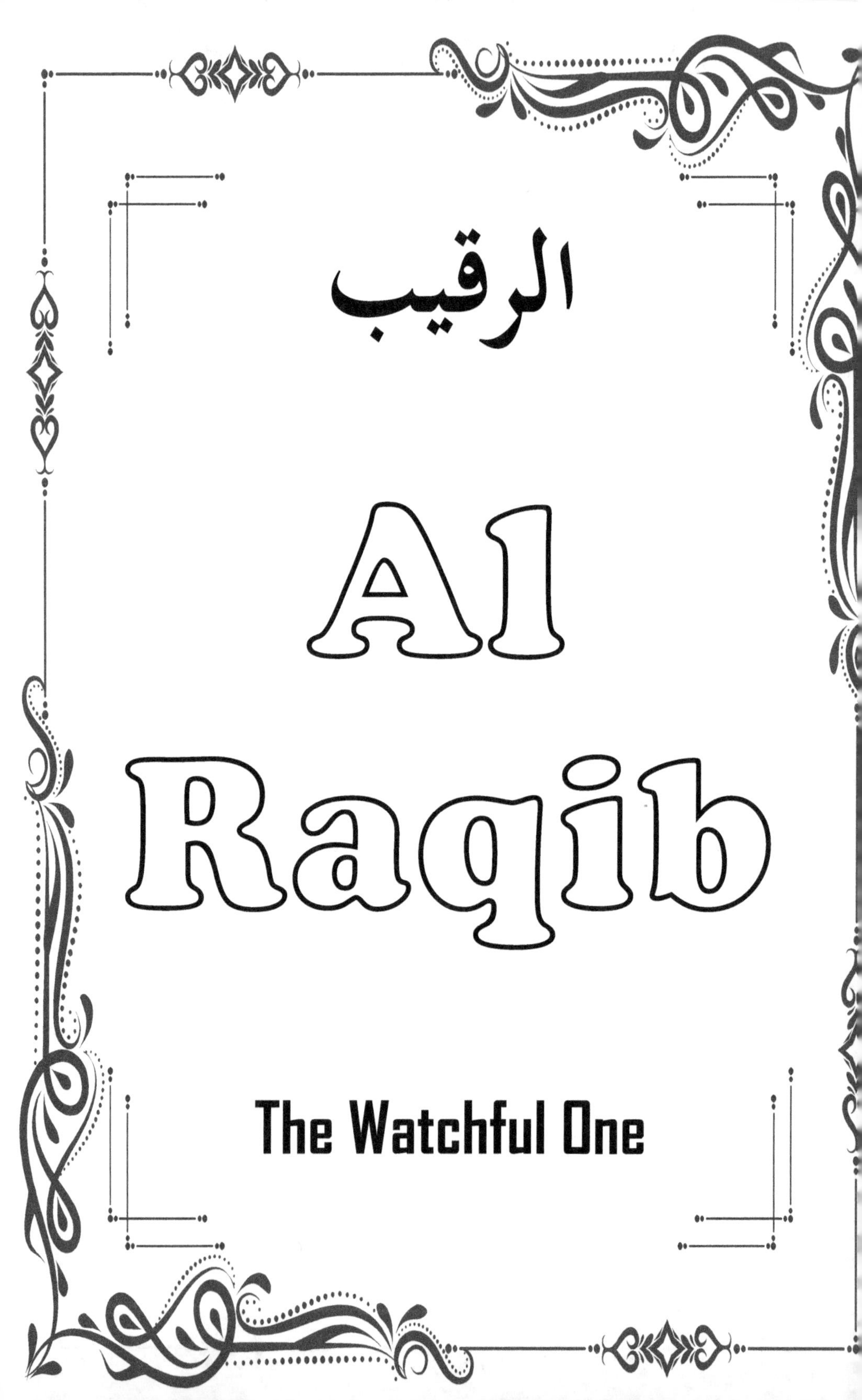
الرقيب

Al
Raqib

The Watchful One

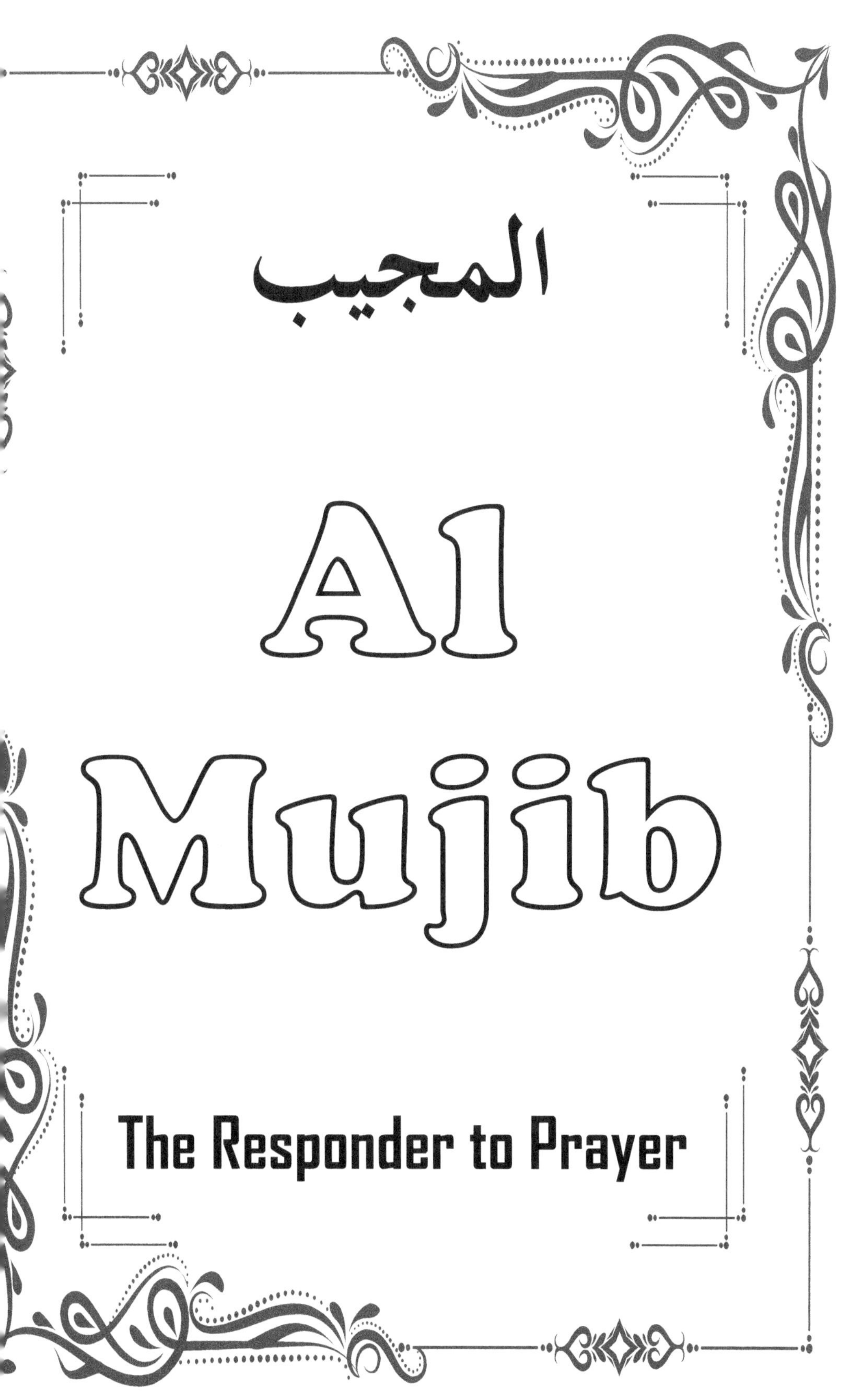

المجيب

Al Mujib

The Responder to Prayer

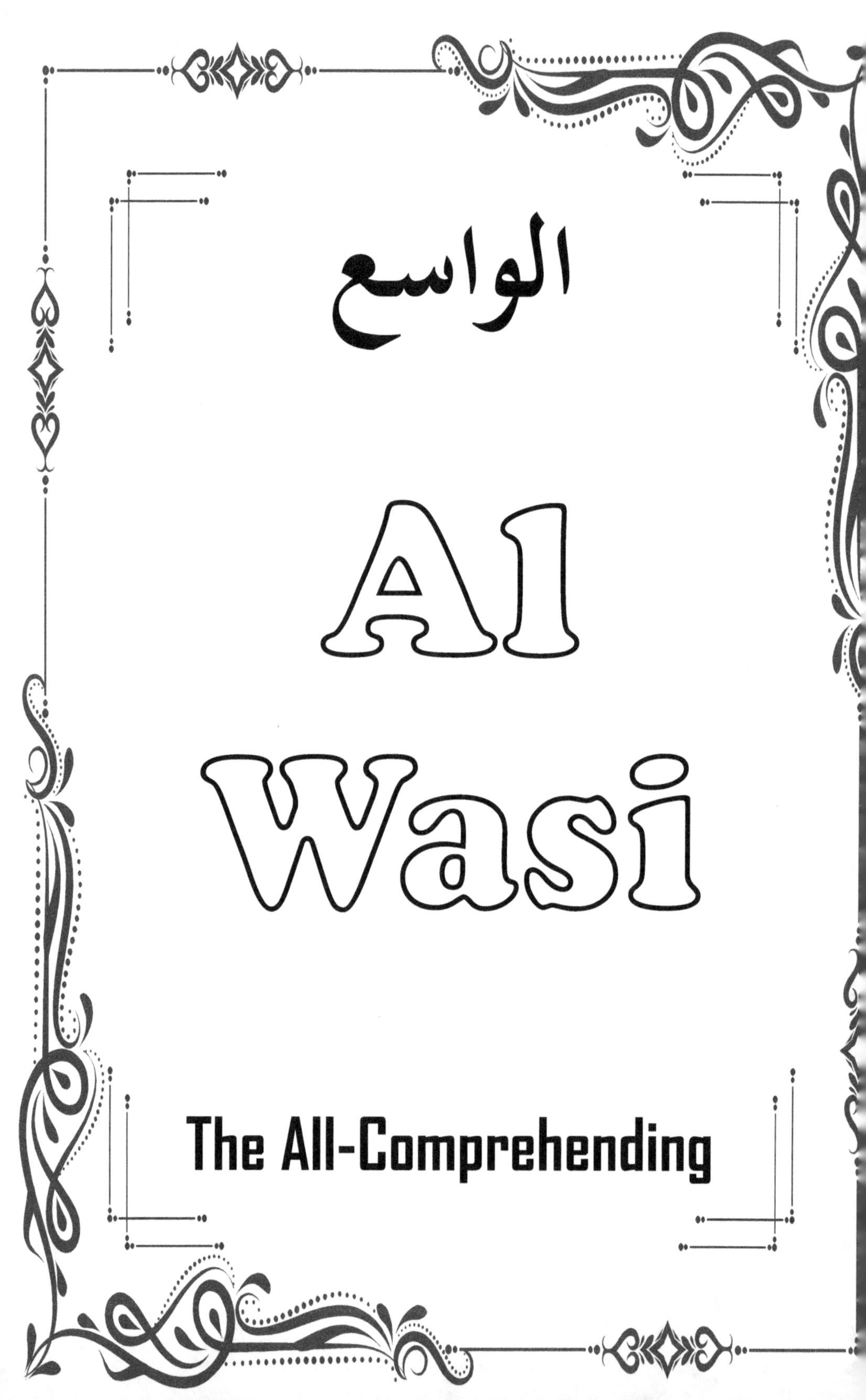

الواسع

Al Wasi

The All-Comprehending

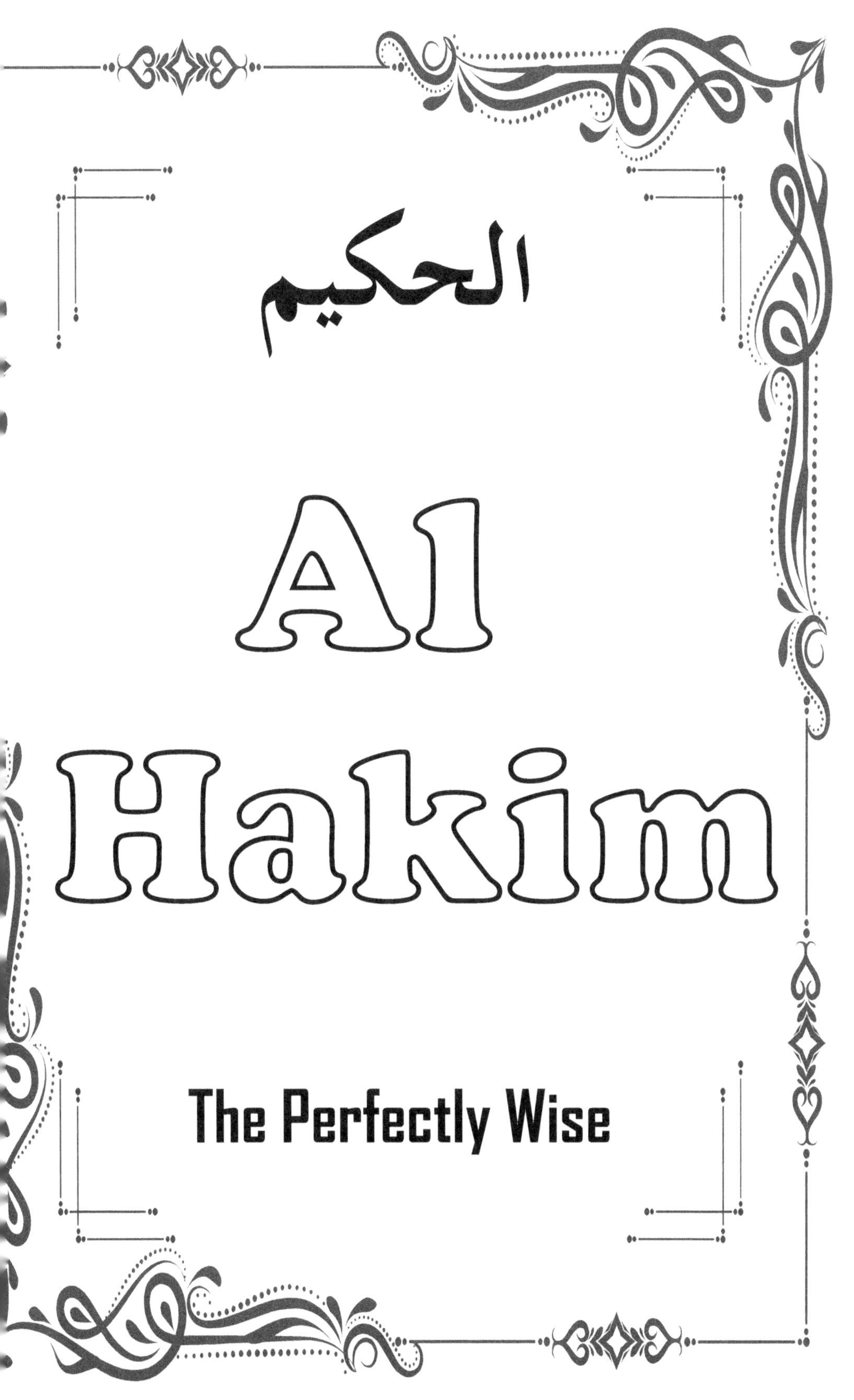

الحكيم

Al Hakim

The Perfectly Wise

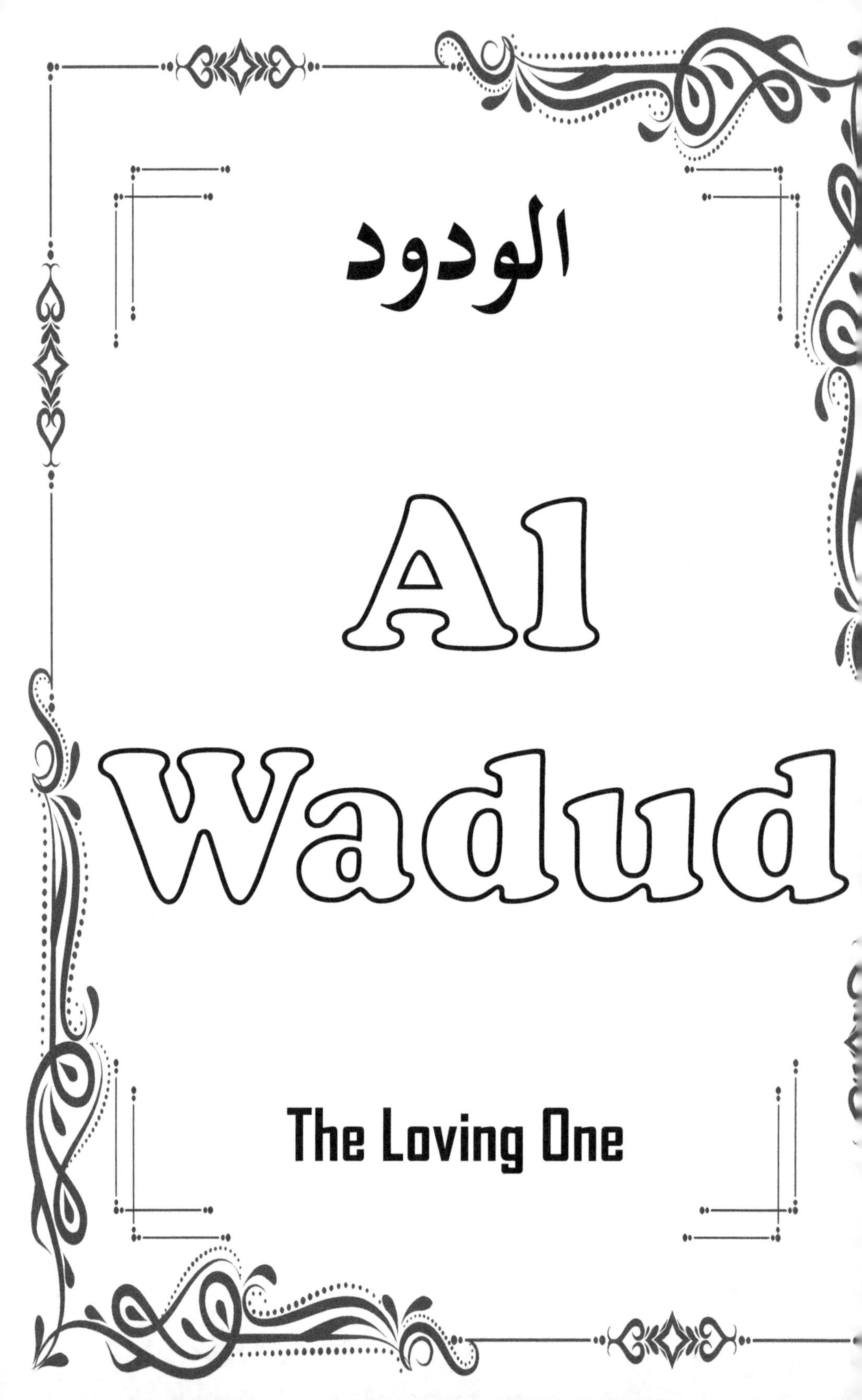

الودود

Al Wadud

The Loving One

المجيد

Al
Majid

The Majestic One

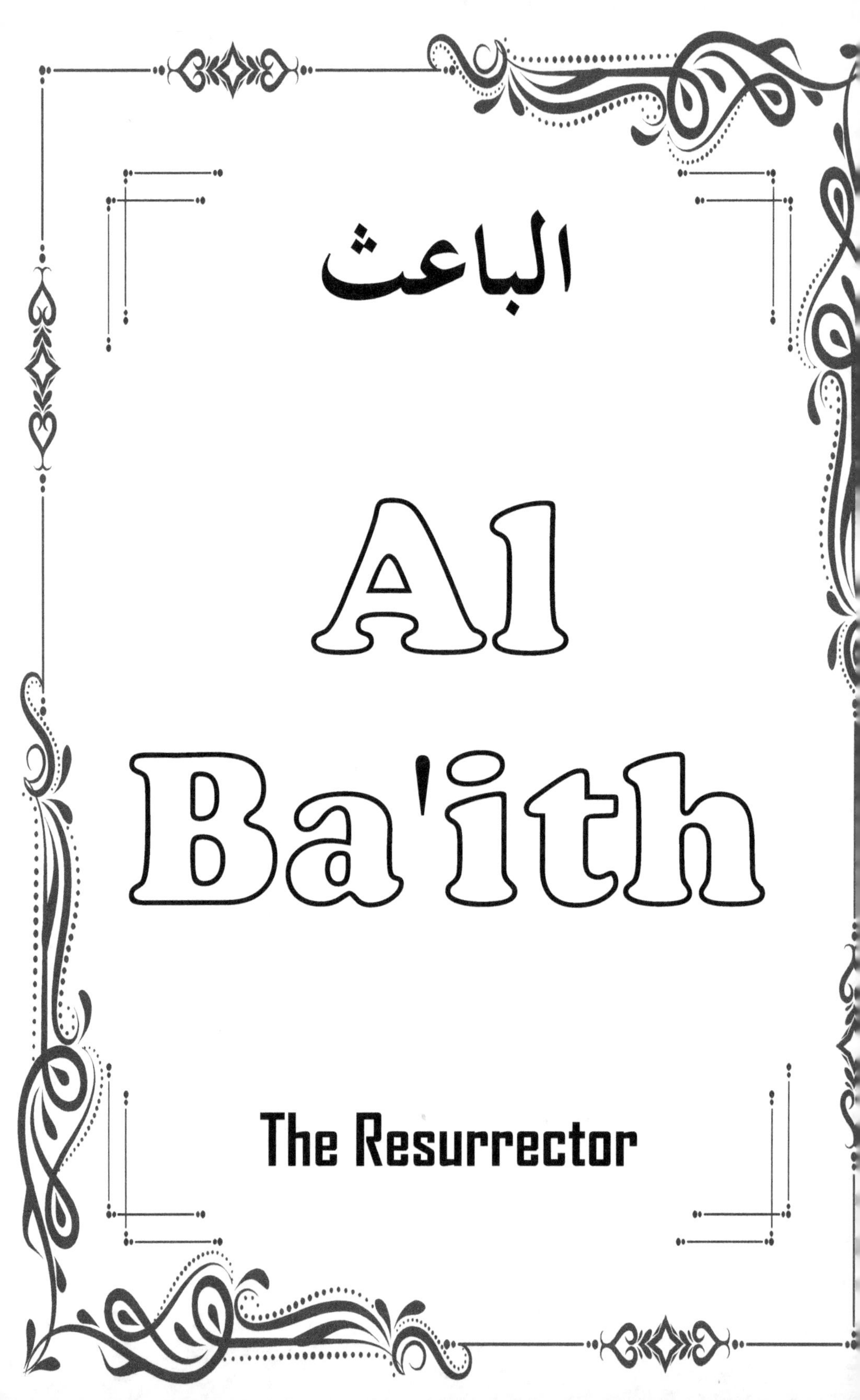

الباعث

Al Ba'ith

The Resurrector

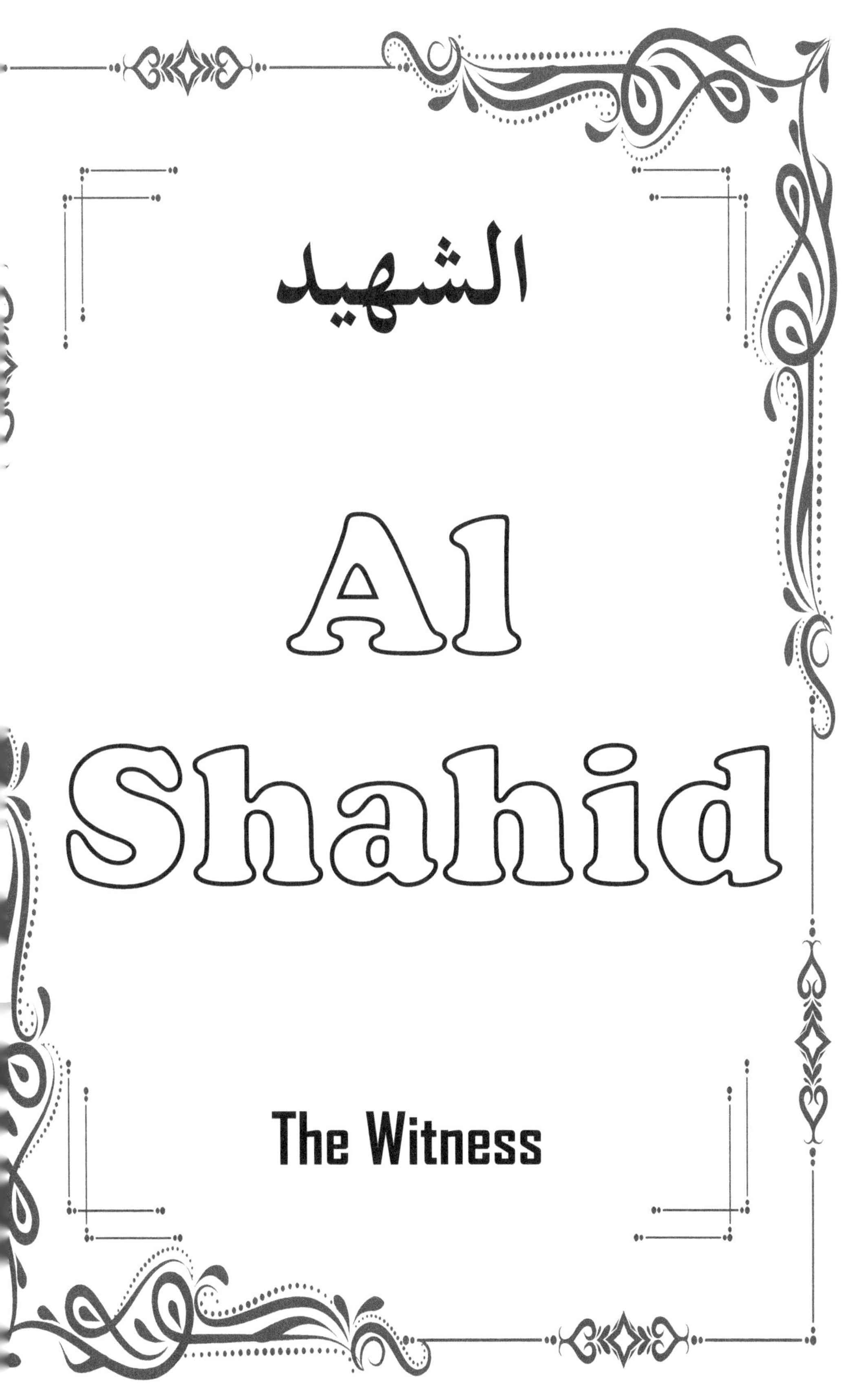

الشهيد

Al Shahid

The Witness

الحق

Al
Haqq

The Truth

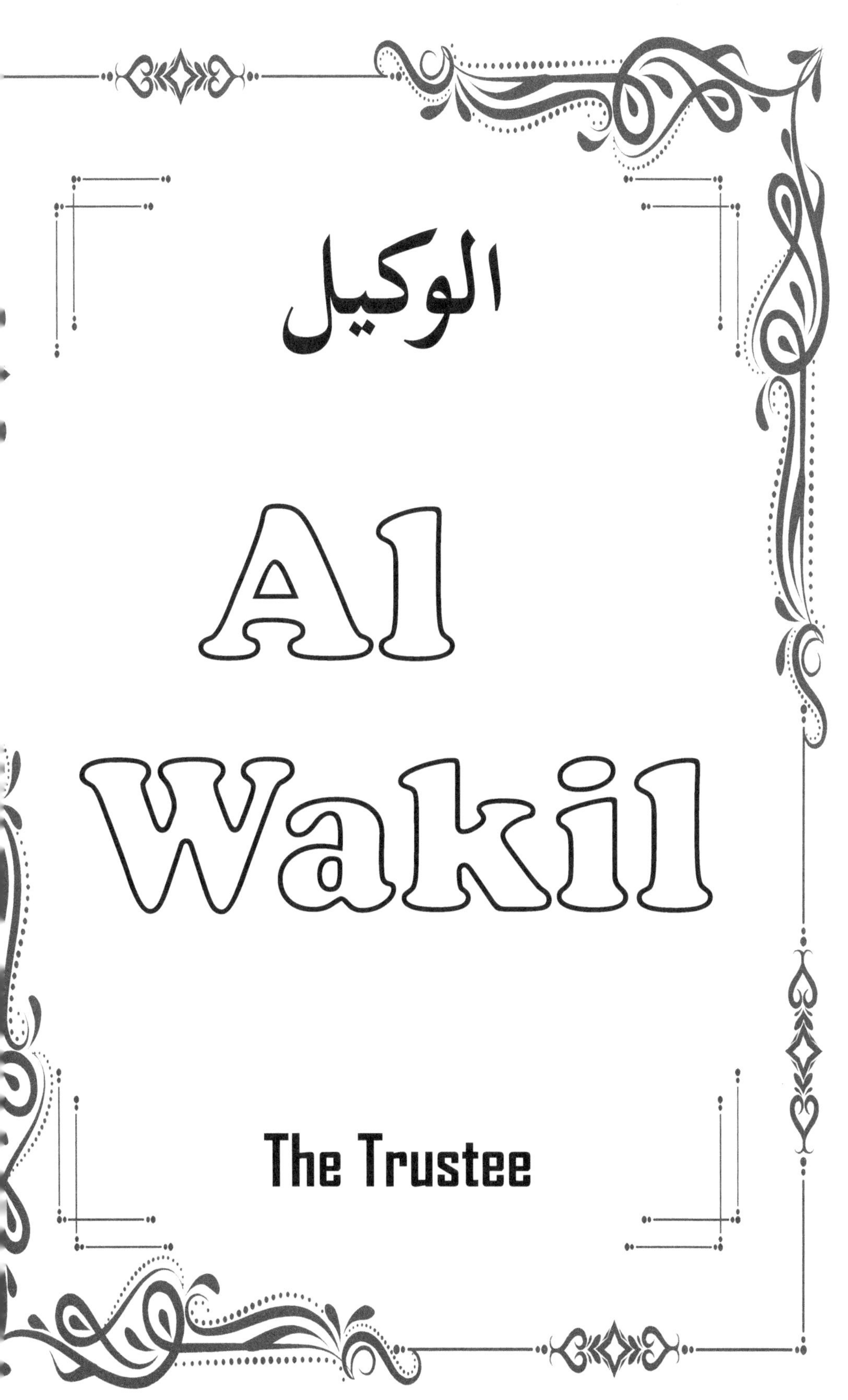

الوكيل

Al Wakil

The Trustee

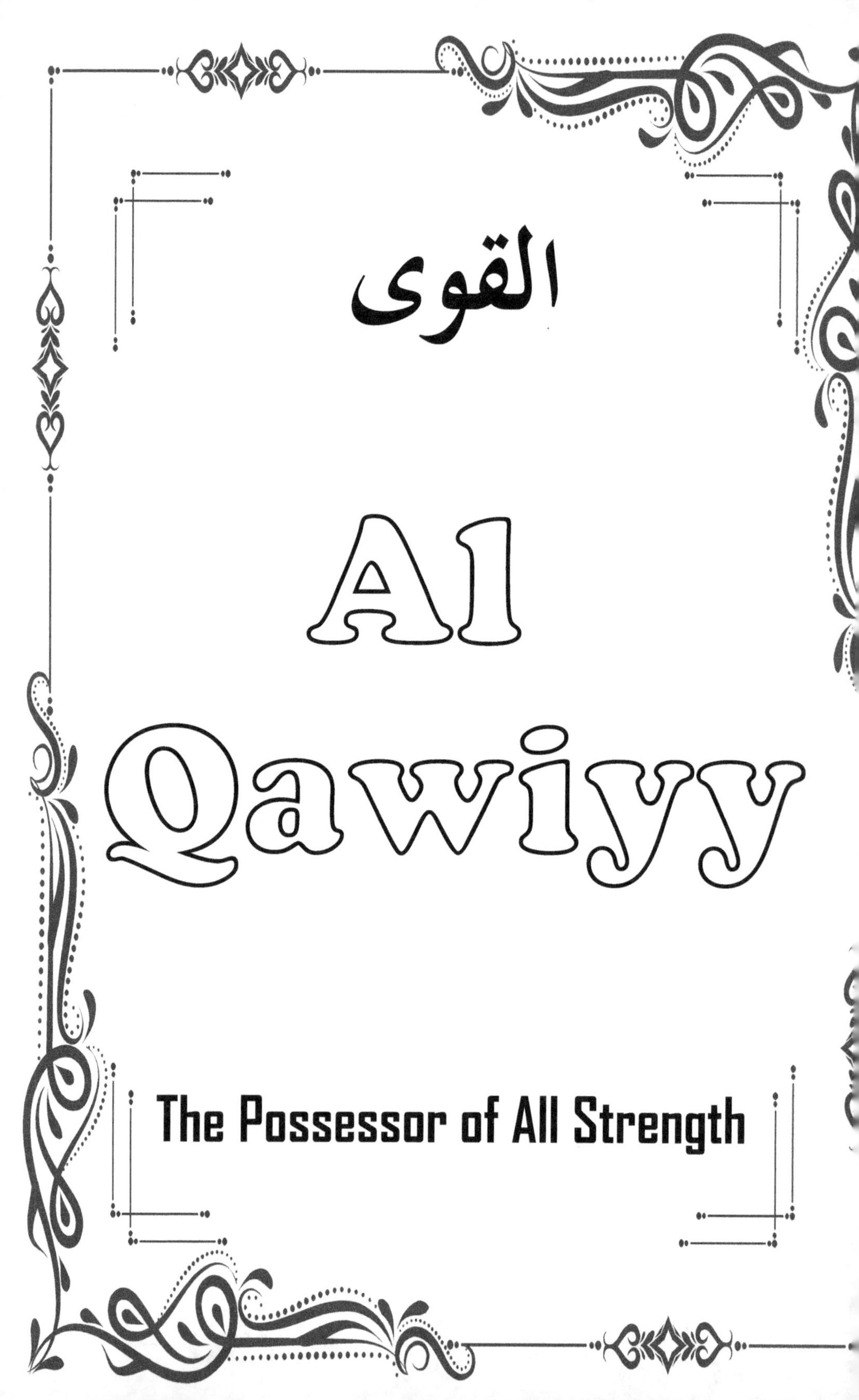

القوى

Al Qawiyy

The Possessor of All Strength

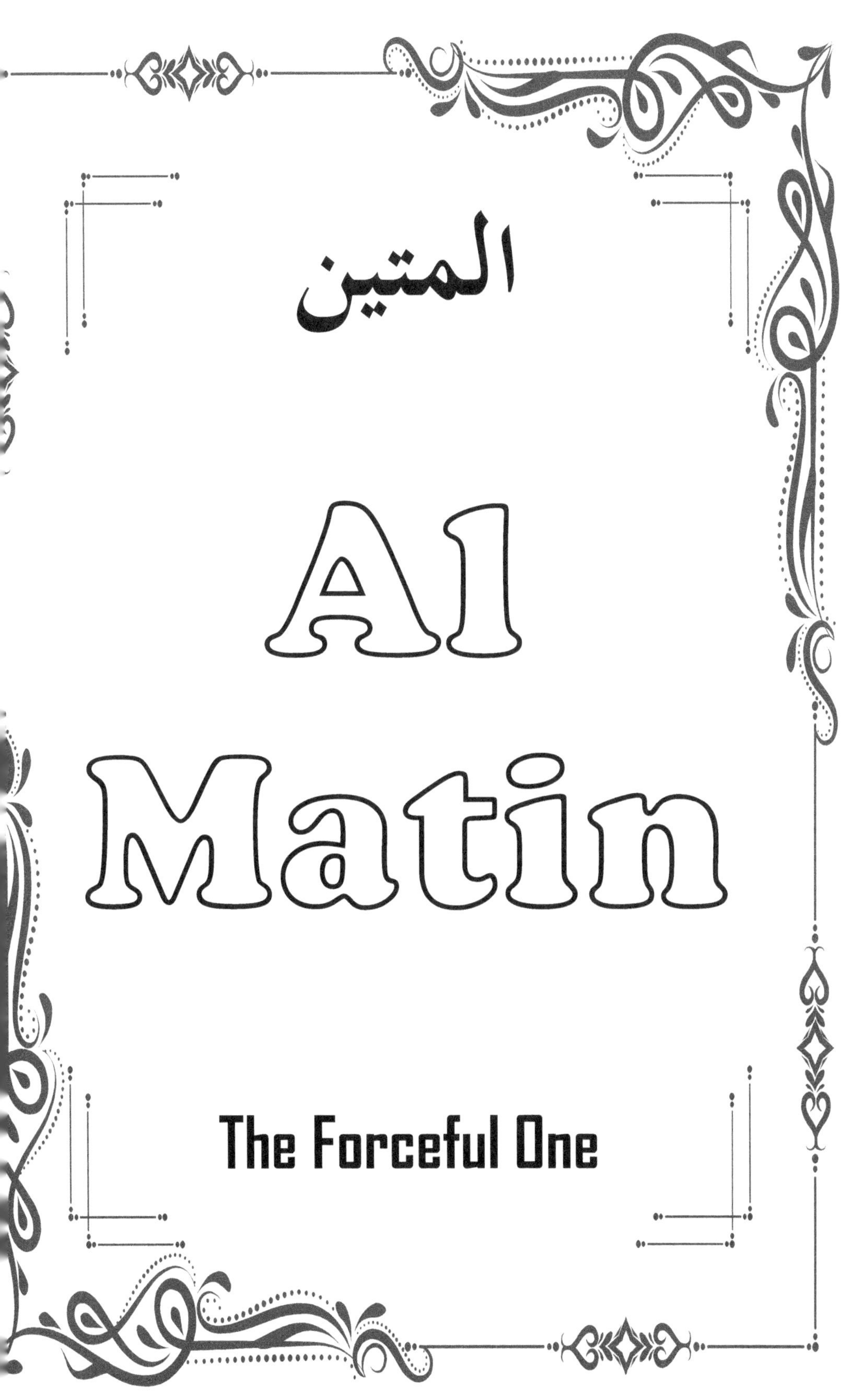

المتين

Al Matin

The Forceful One

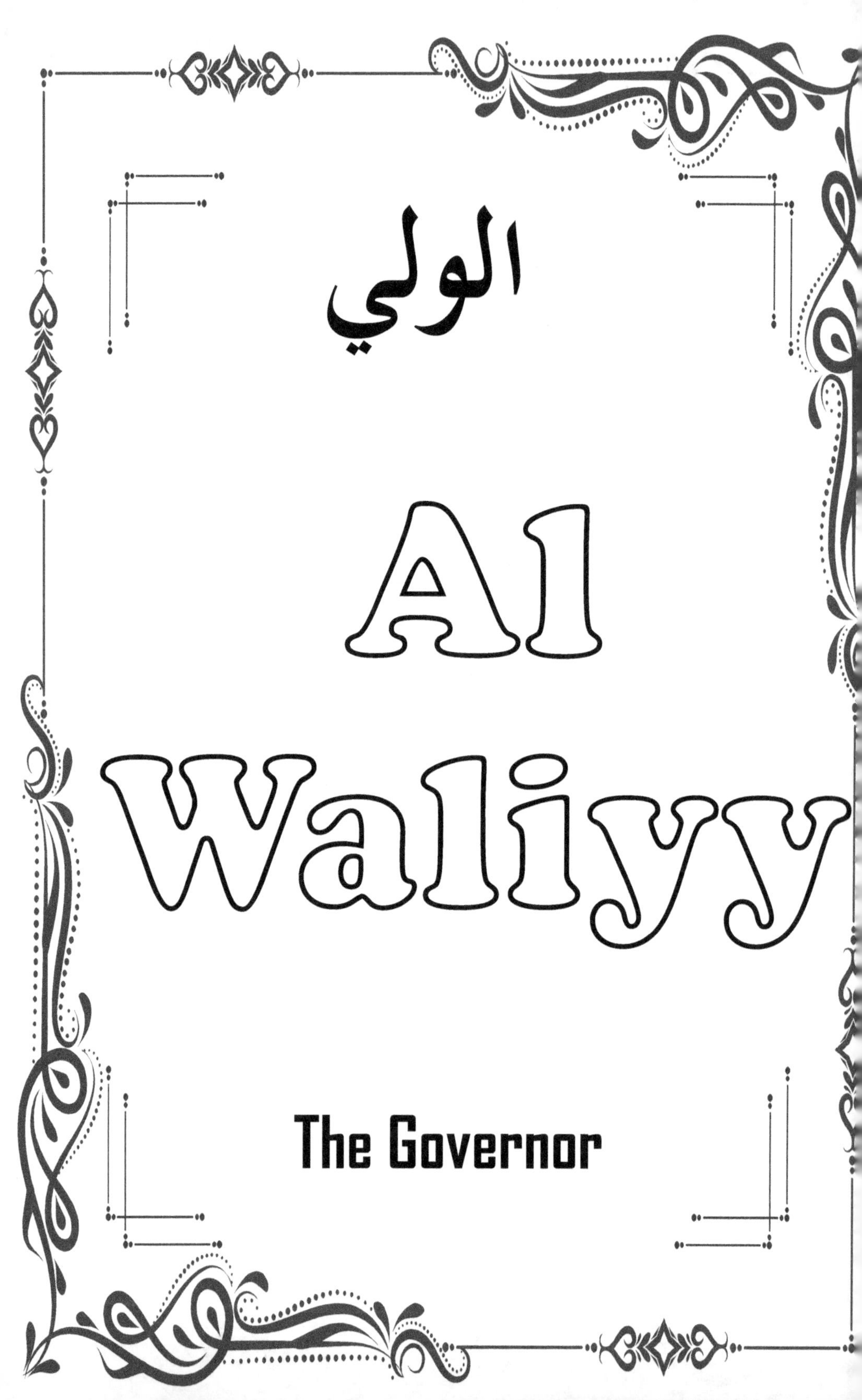

الولي

Al Waliyy

The Governor

الحميد

Al Hamid

The Praised One

المحصى

Al Muhsi

The Appraiser

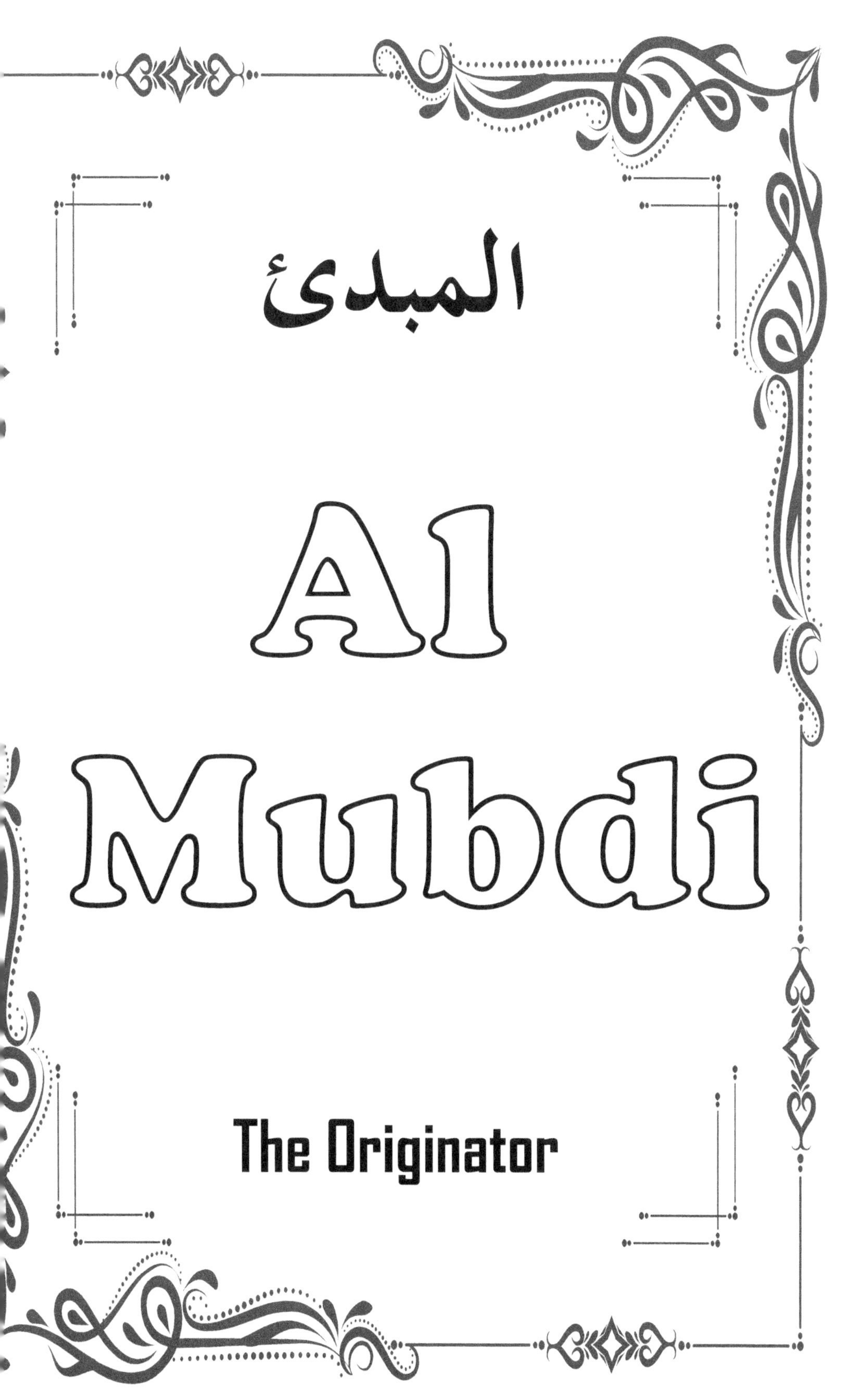

المبدئ

Al
Mubdi

The Originator

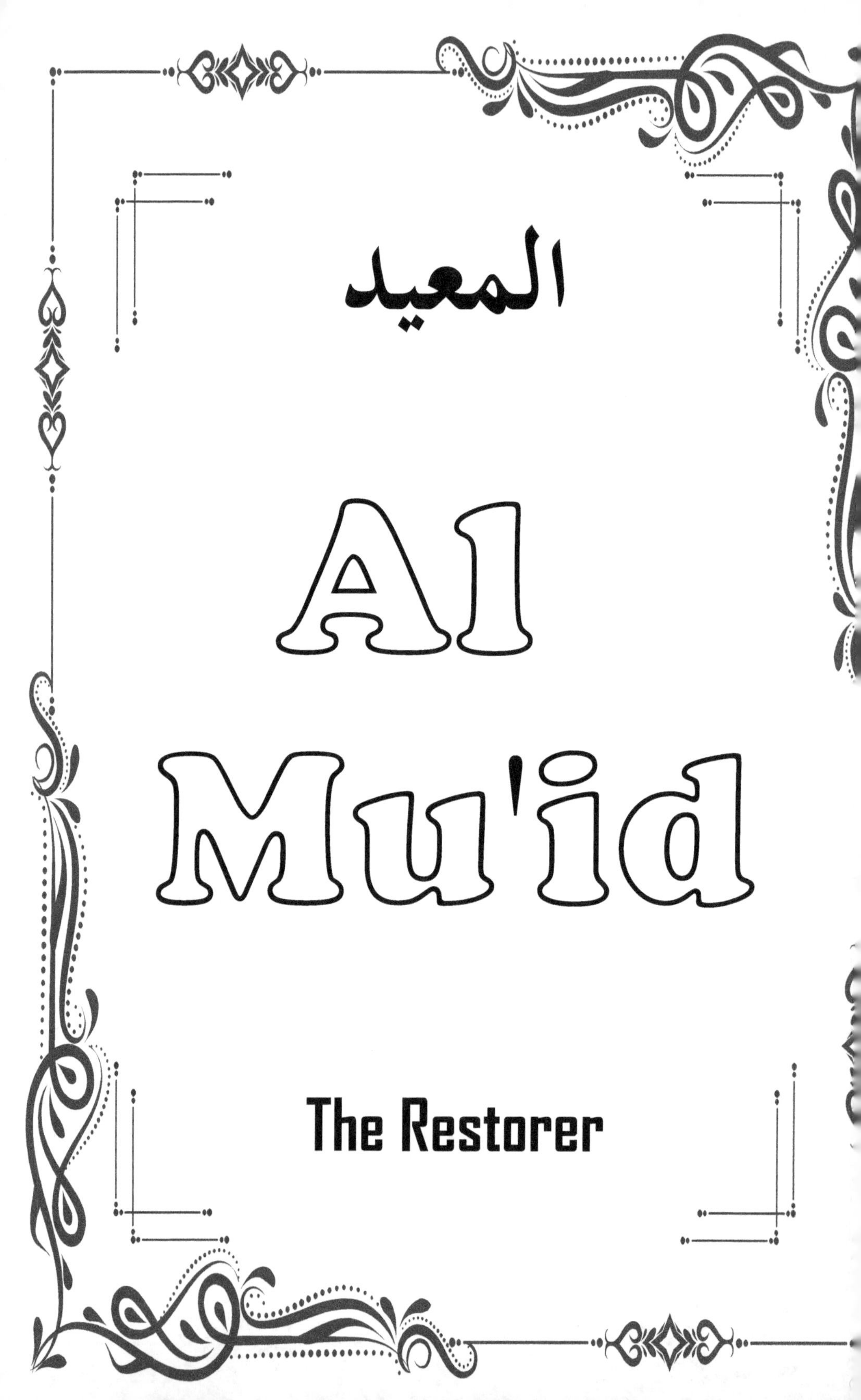

المعيد

Al
Mu'id

The Restorer

المحيي

Al Muhyi

The Giver of Life

المميت

Al Mumit

The Taker of Life

الحي

Al Hayy

The Ever Living One

القيوم

Al
Qayyum

The Self-Existing One

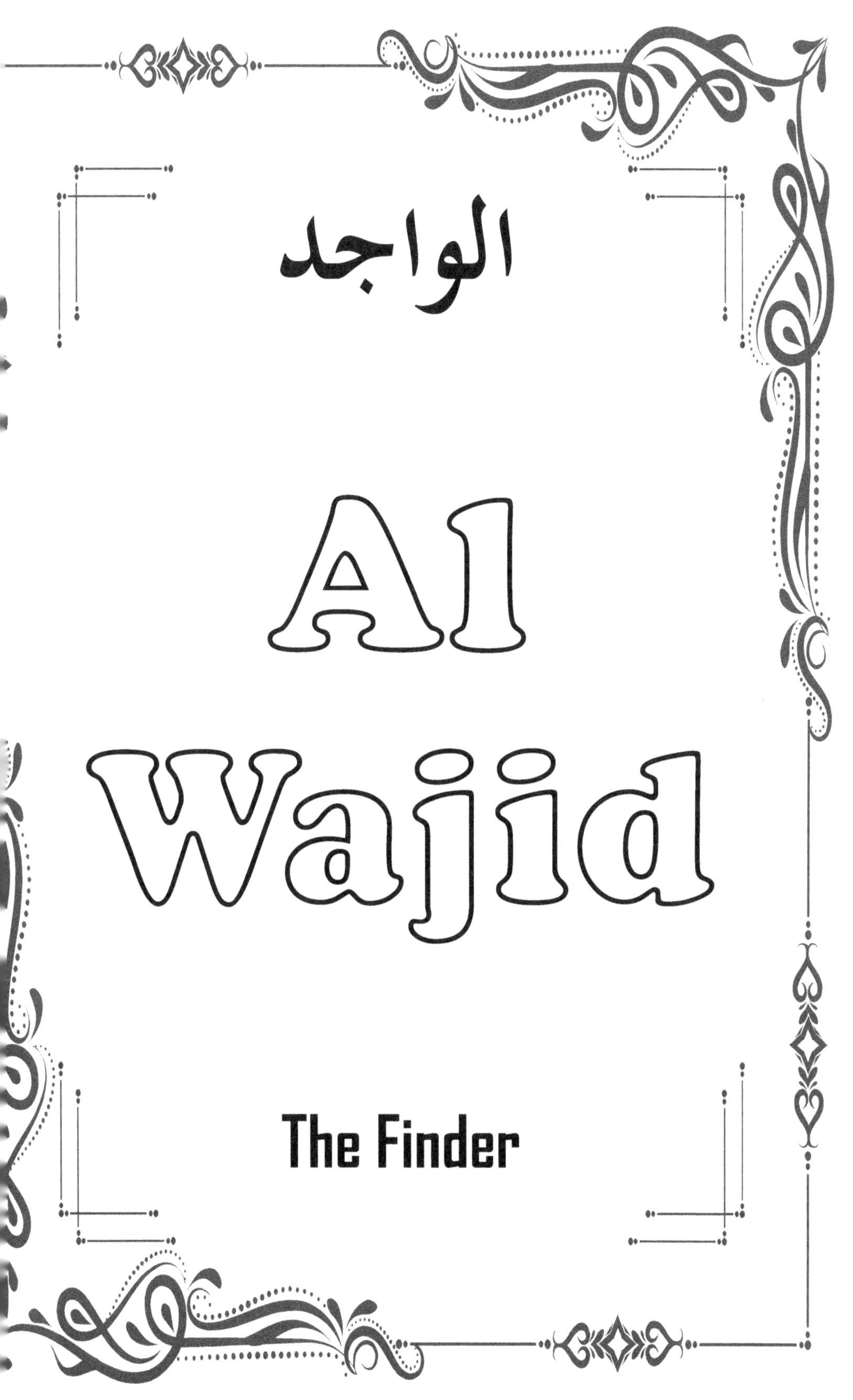

الواجد

Al Wajid

The Finder

الماجد

Al Majid

The Glorious

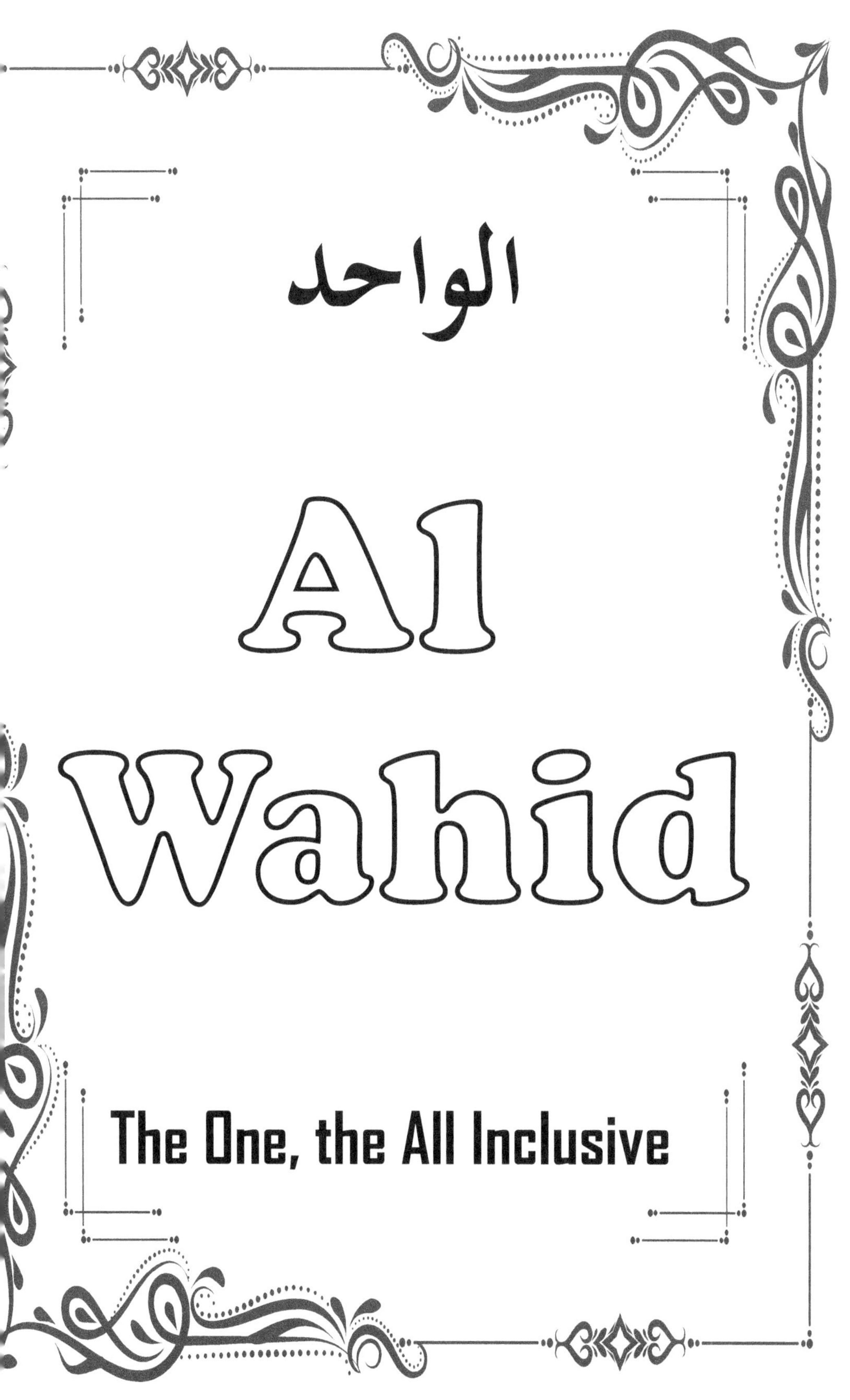

الواحد

Al Wahid

The One, the All Inclusive

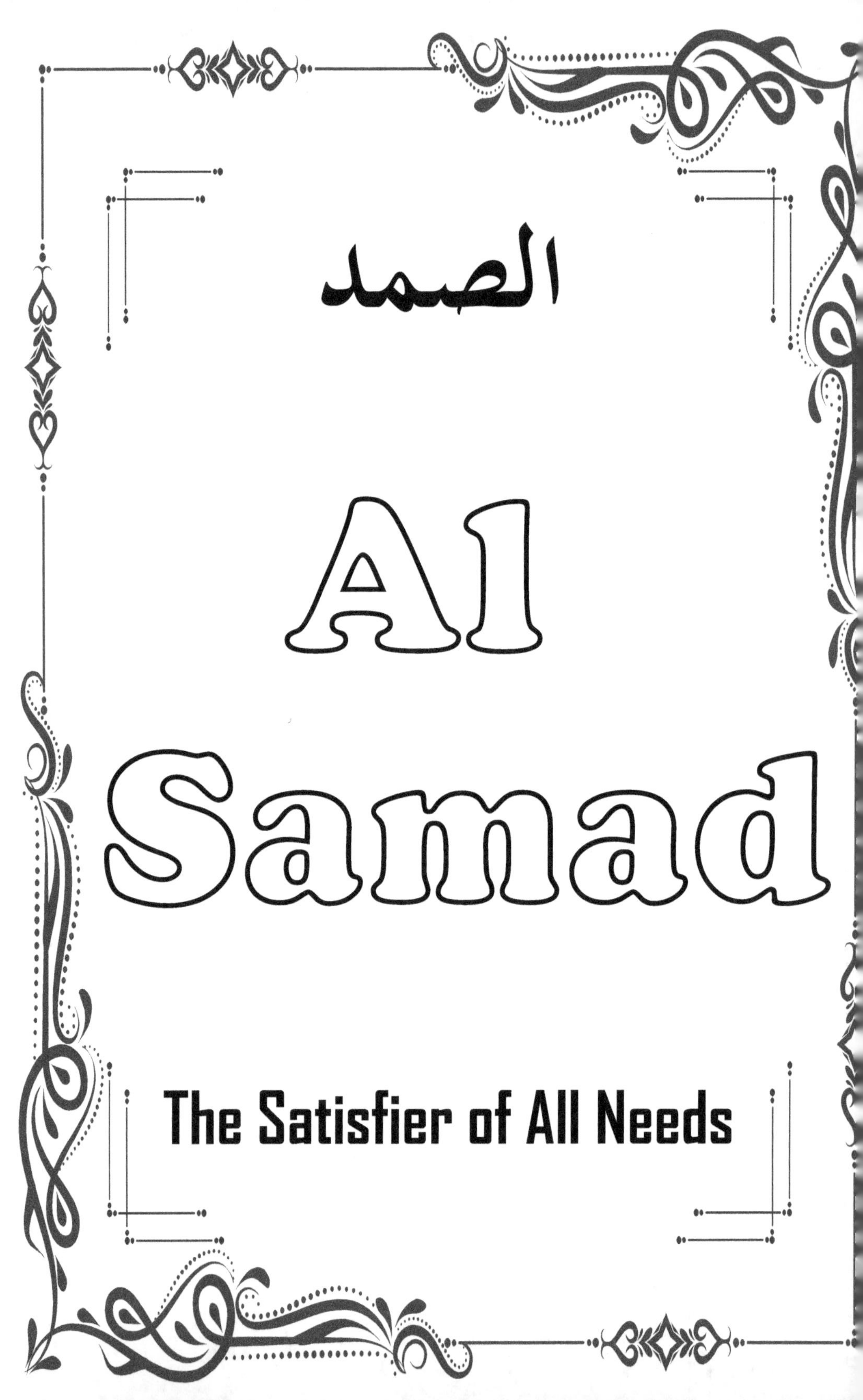

الصمد

Al
Samad

The Satisfier of All Needs

القادر
Al Qadir
The All Powerful

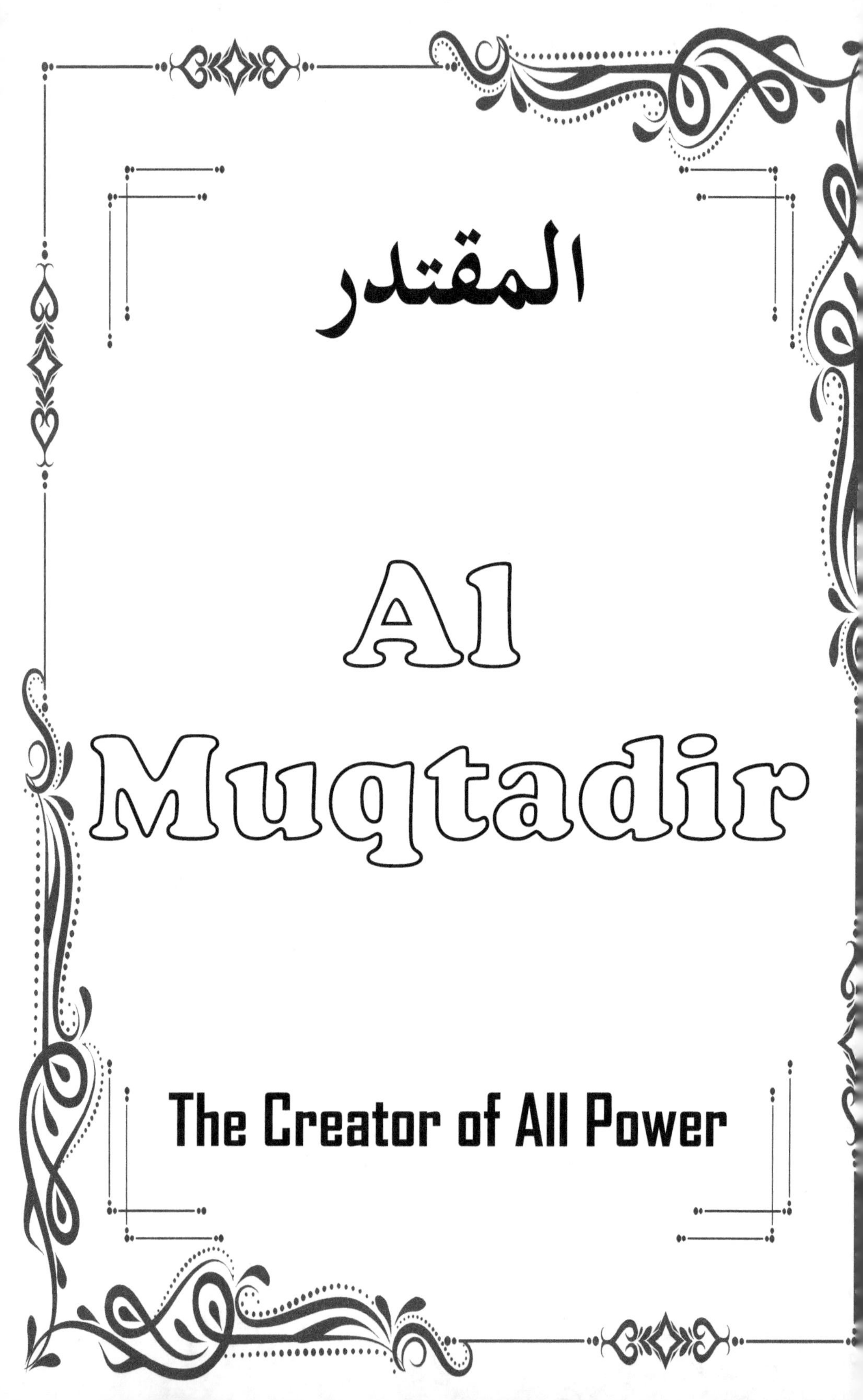

المقتدر

Al
Muqtadir

The Creator of All Power

المقدم

Al
Muqaddim

The Expediter

المؤخر

Al Mu'akhkhir

The Delayer

الأول

Al
Awwal

The First

الآخر

Al Akhir

The Last

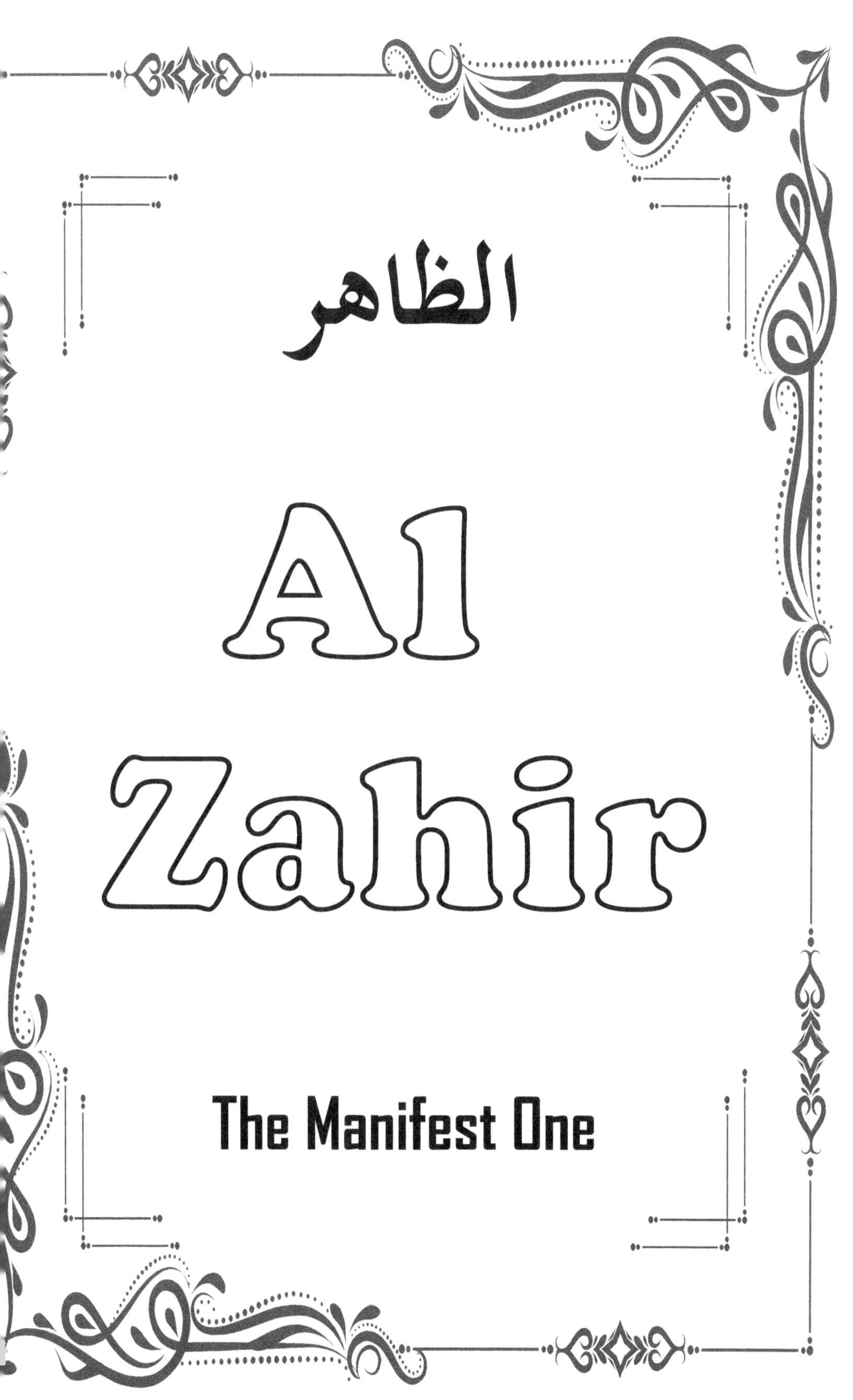

الظاهر

Al Zahir

The Manifest One

الباطن
Al Batin
The Hidden One

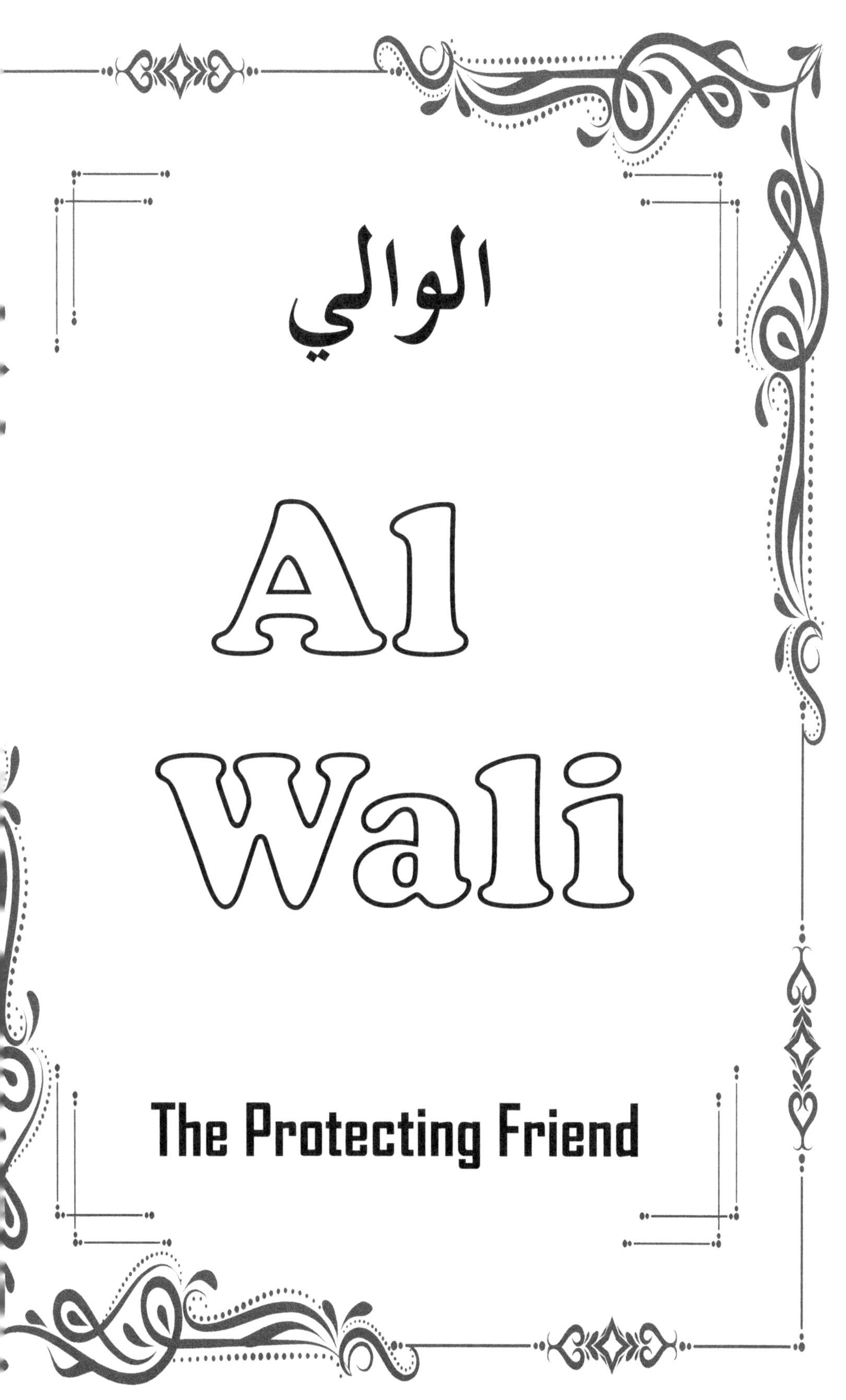

الوالي

Al
Wali

The Protecting Friend

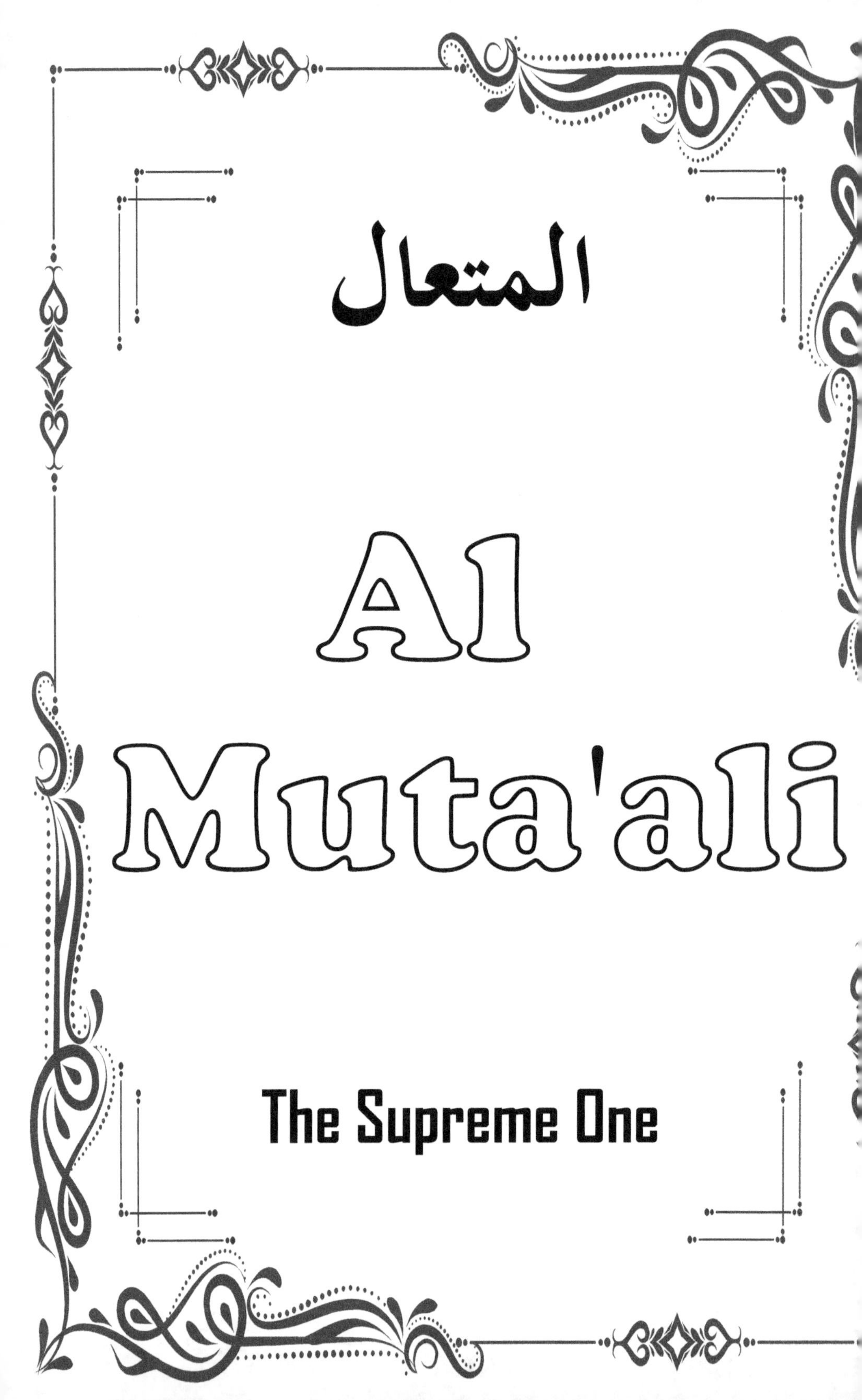

المتعال

Al Muta'ali

The Supreme One

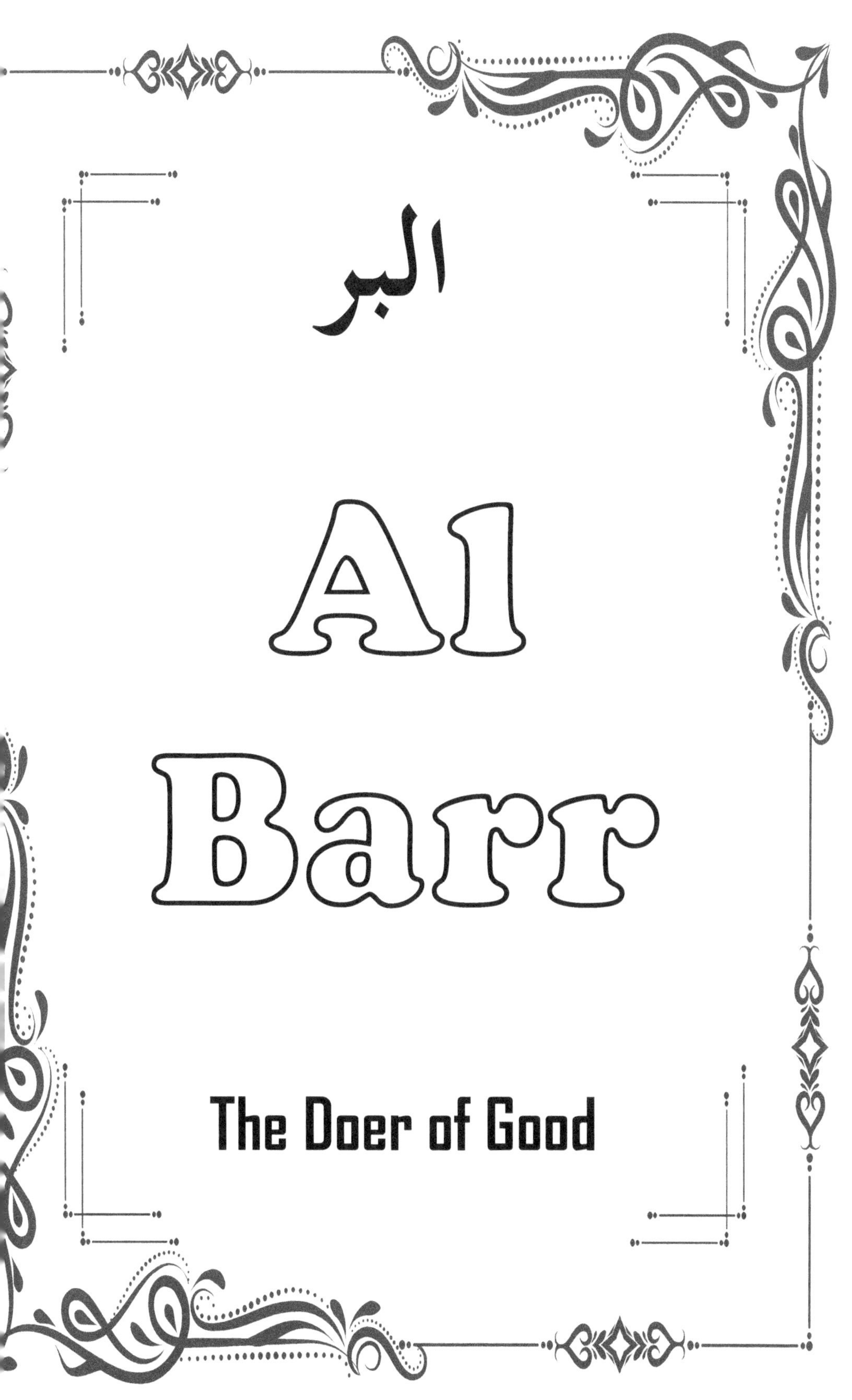

البر

Al
Barr

The Doer of Good

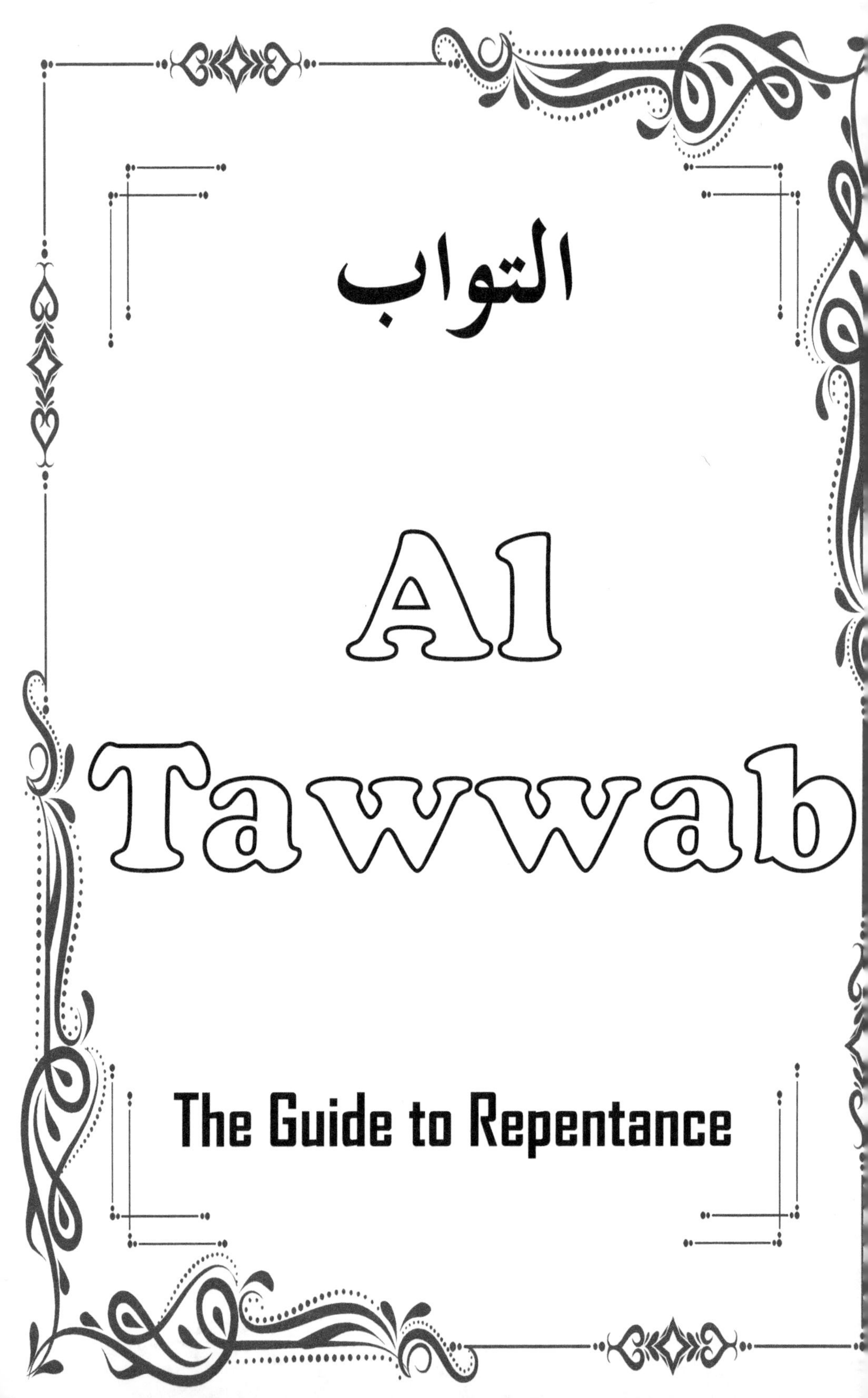

التواب

Al Tawwwab

The Guide to Repentance

المنتقم

Al Muntaqim

The Avenger

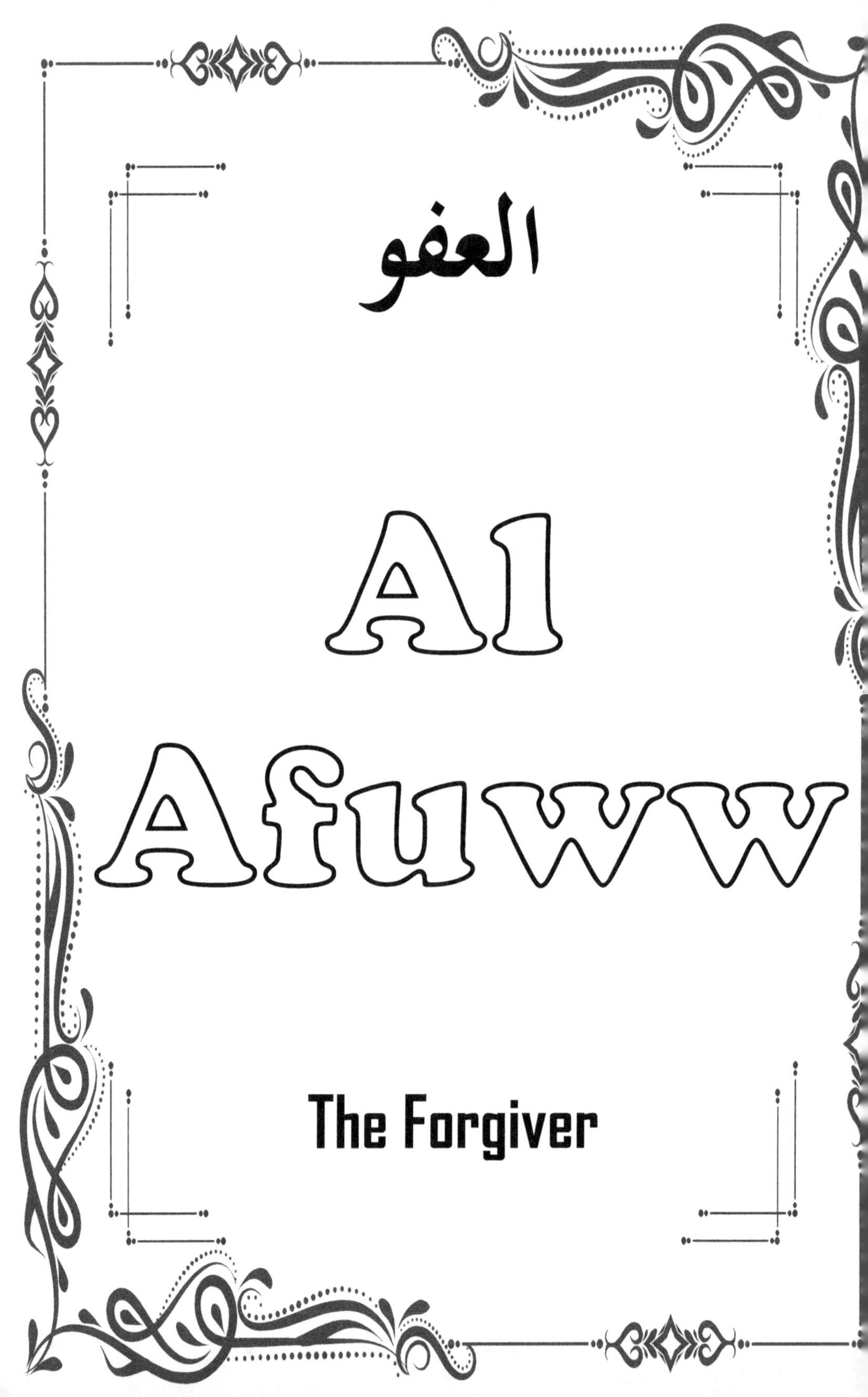

العفو

Al Afuww

The Forgiver

الرؤوف

Al
Ra'uf

The Clement

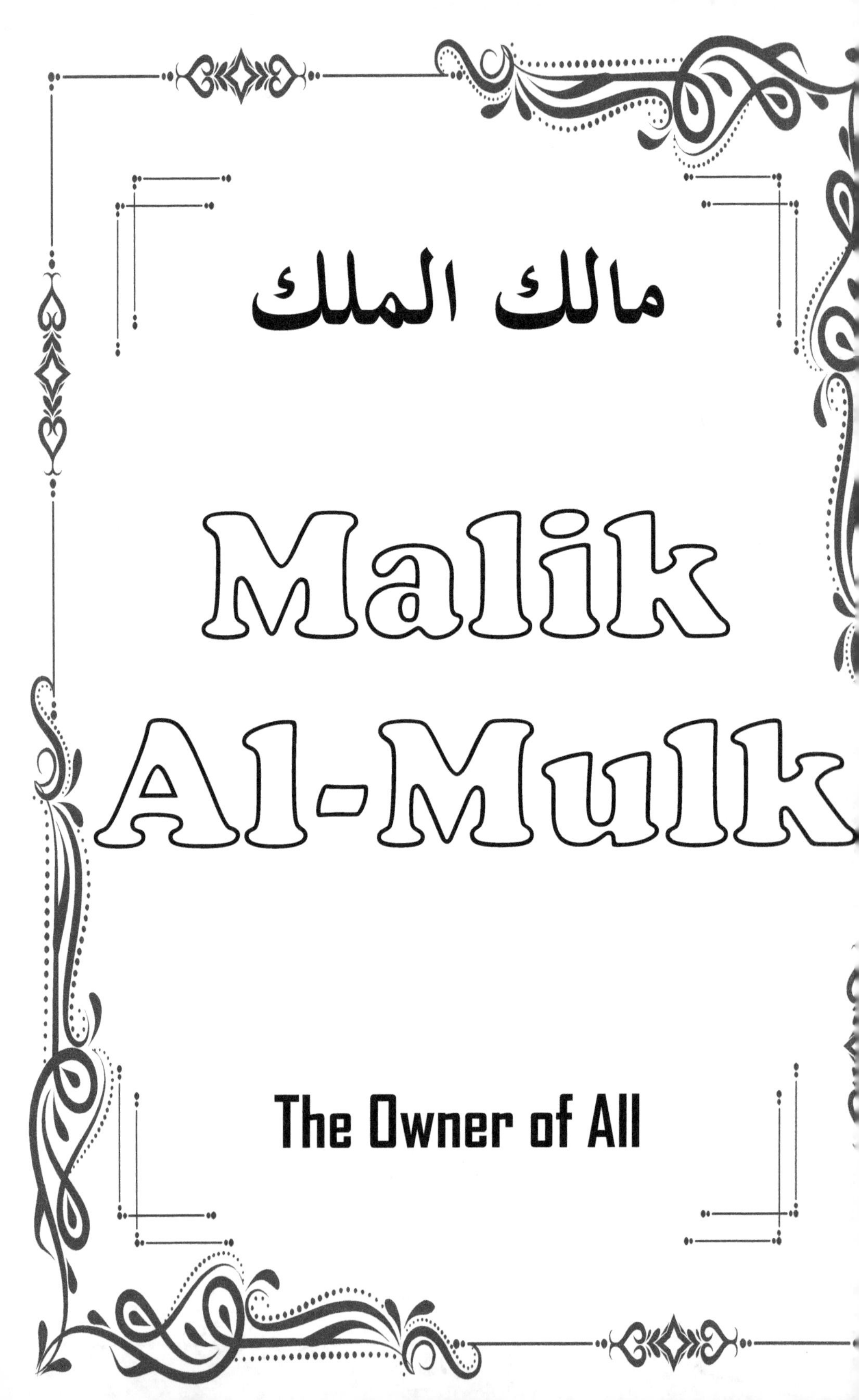

مالك الملك

Malik
Al-Mulk

The Owner of All

ذو الجلال و الإكرام

Dhu-al-Jalal
wa-al-Ikram

The Lord of Majesty and Bounty

المقسط

Al Muqsit

The Equitable One

الجامع

Al Jami'

The Gatherer

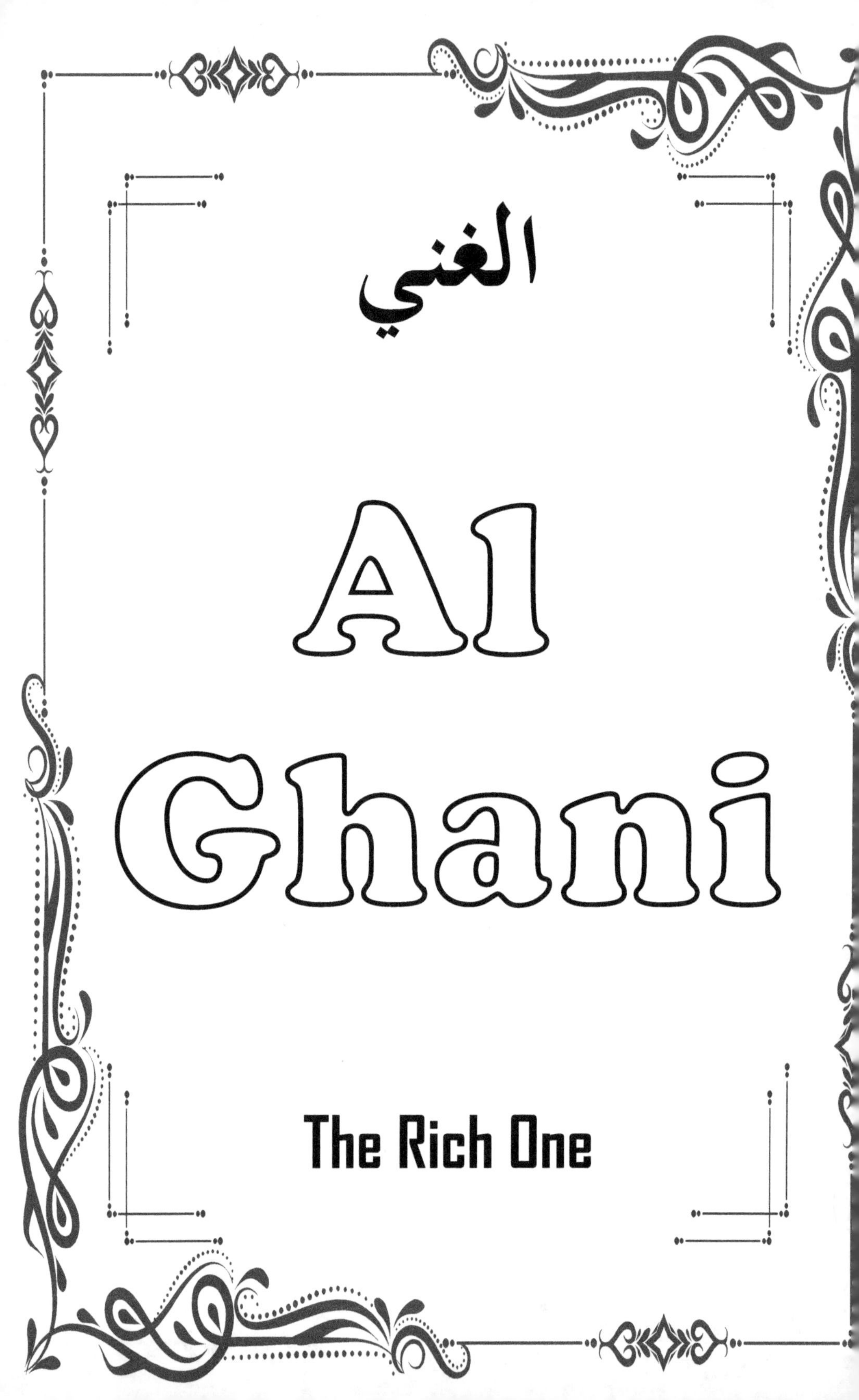

الغني

Al Ghani

The Rich One

المغني
Al Mughni
The Enricher

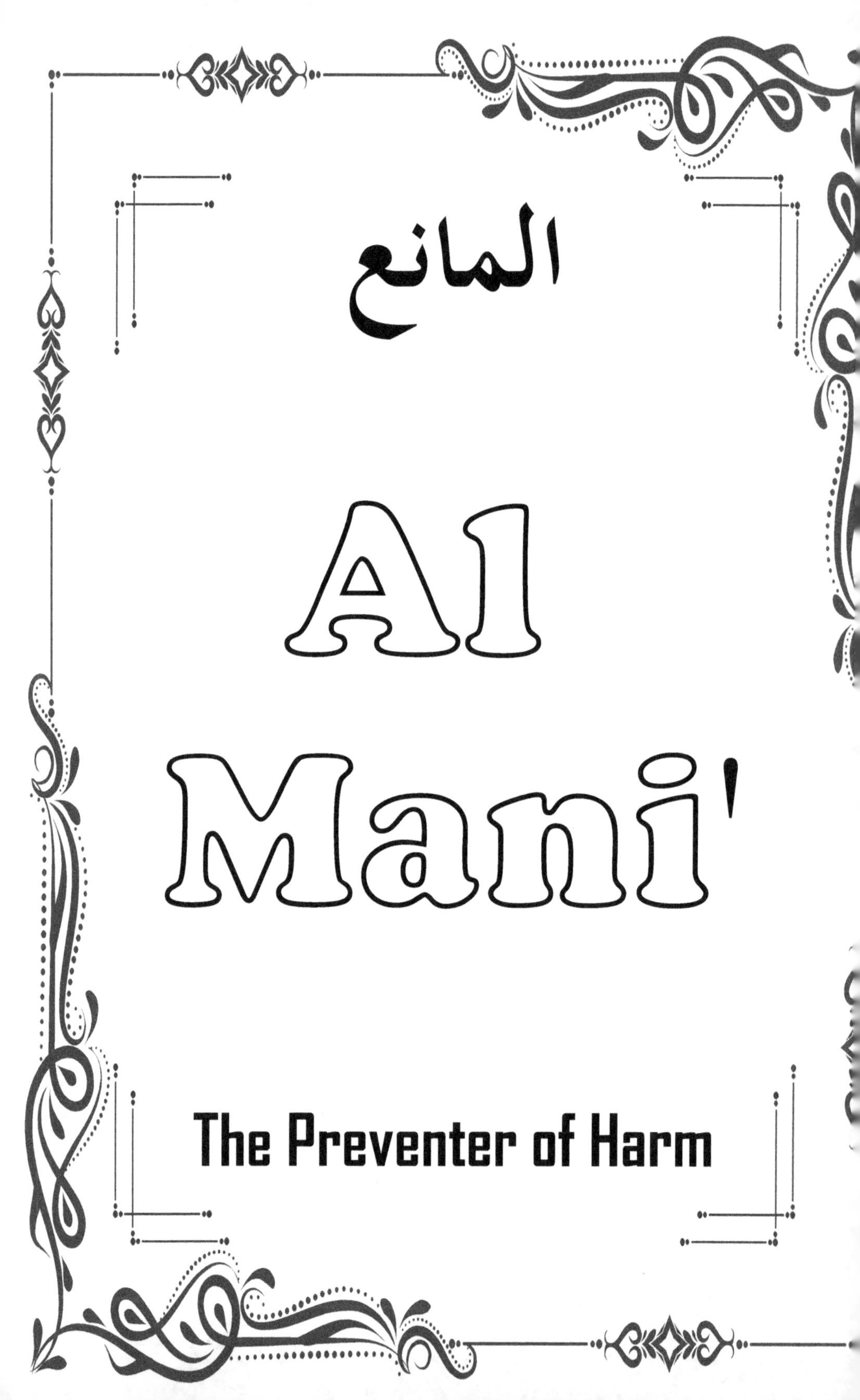
المانع

Al
Mani'

The Preventer of Harm

الضار

Al
Darr

The Creator of The Harmful

النافع

Al
Nafi'

The Creator of Good

النور

Al
Nur

The Greatest Name

الهادي

Al Hadi

The Guide

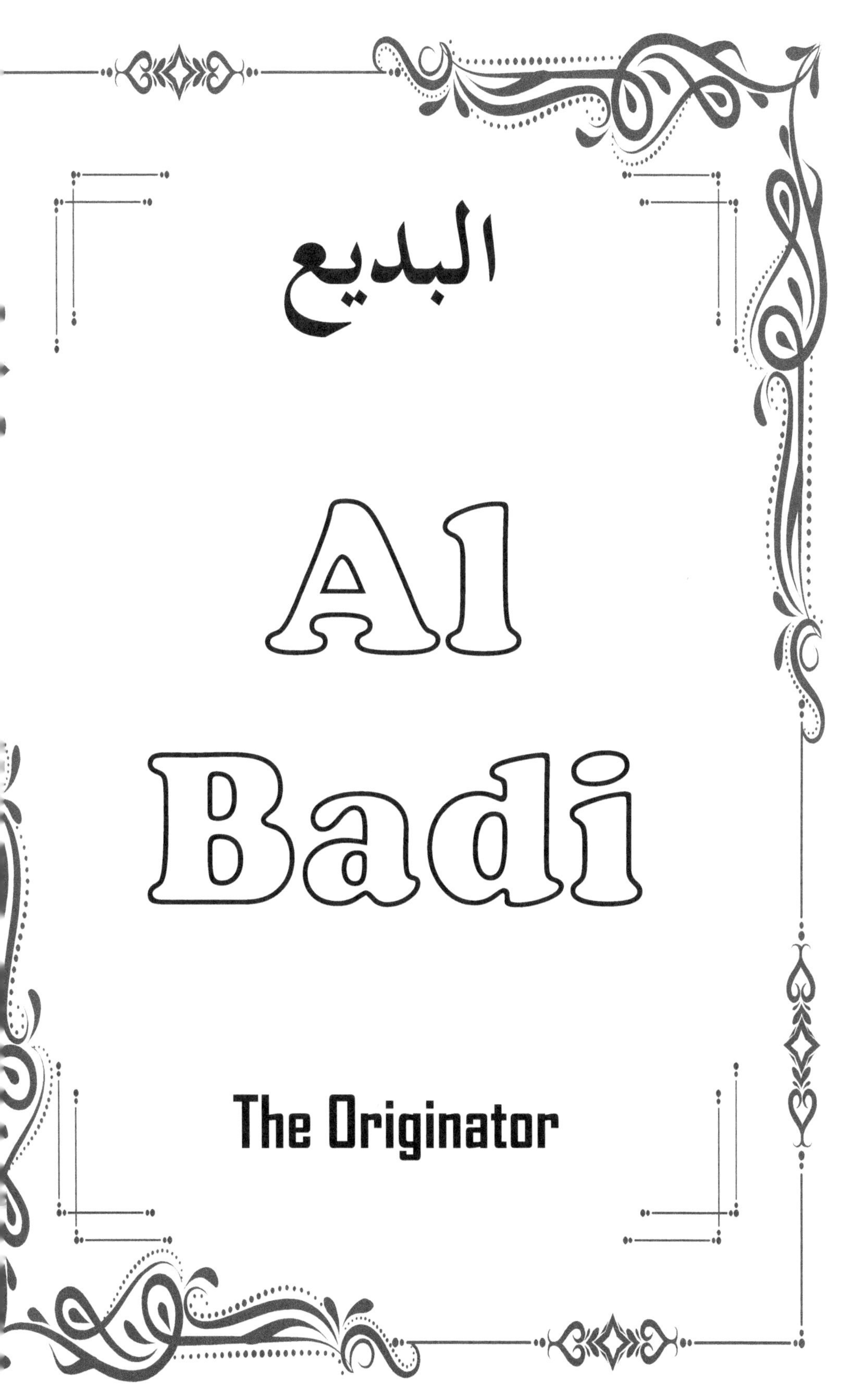

البديع

Al
Badi

The Originator

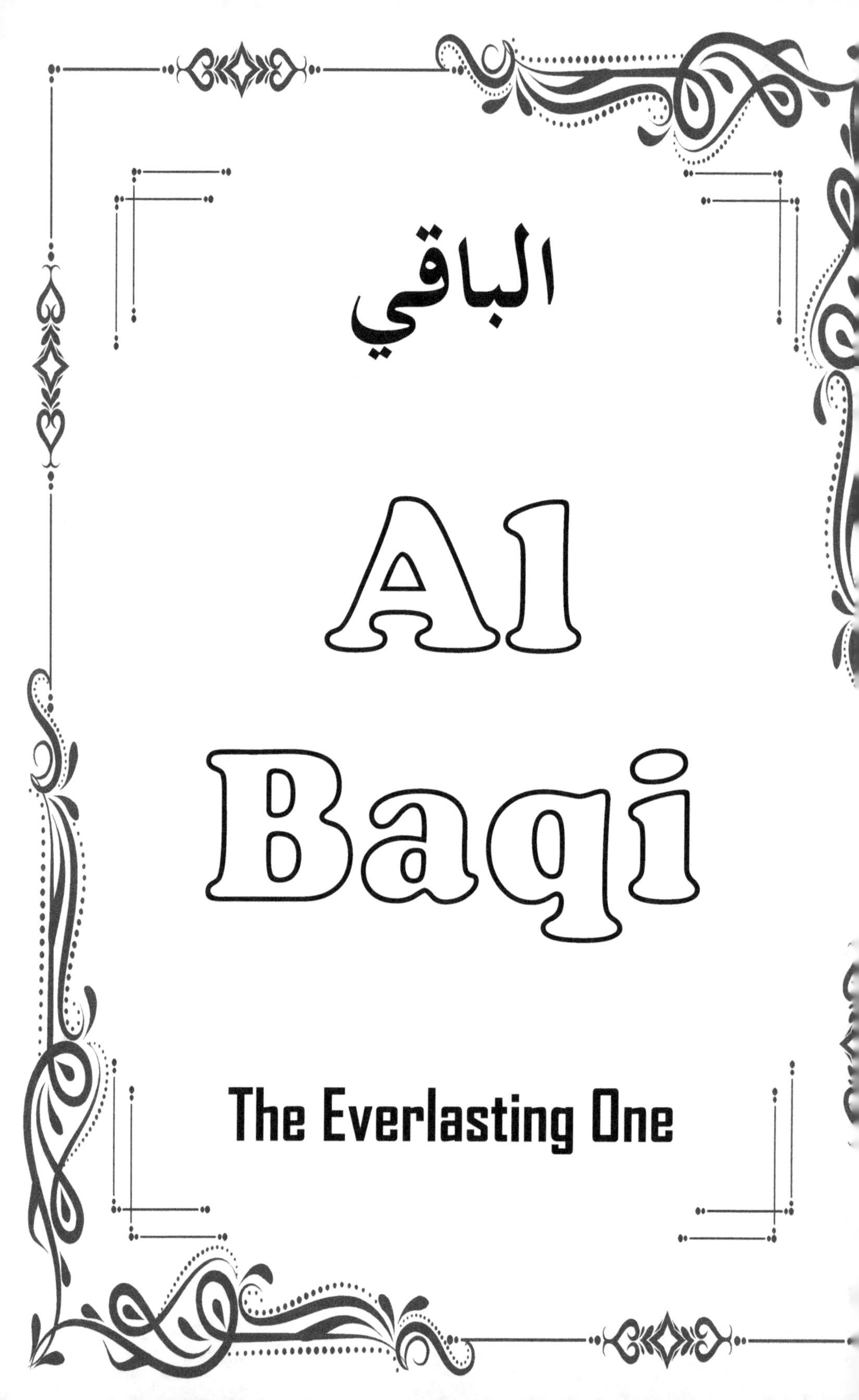
الباقي
Al
Baqi
The Everlasting One

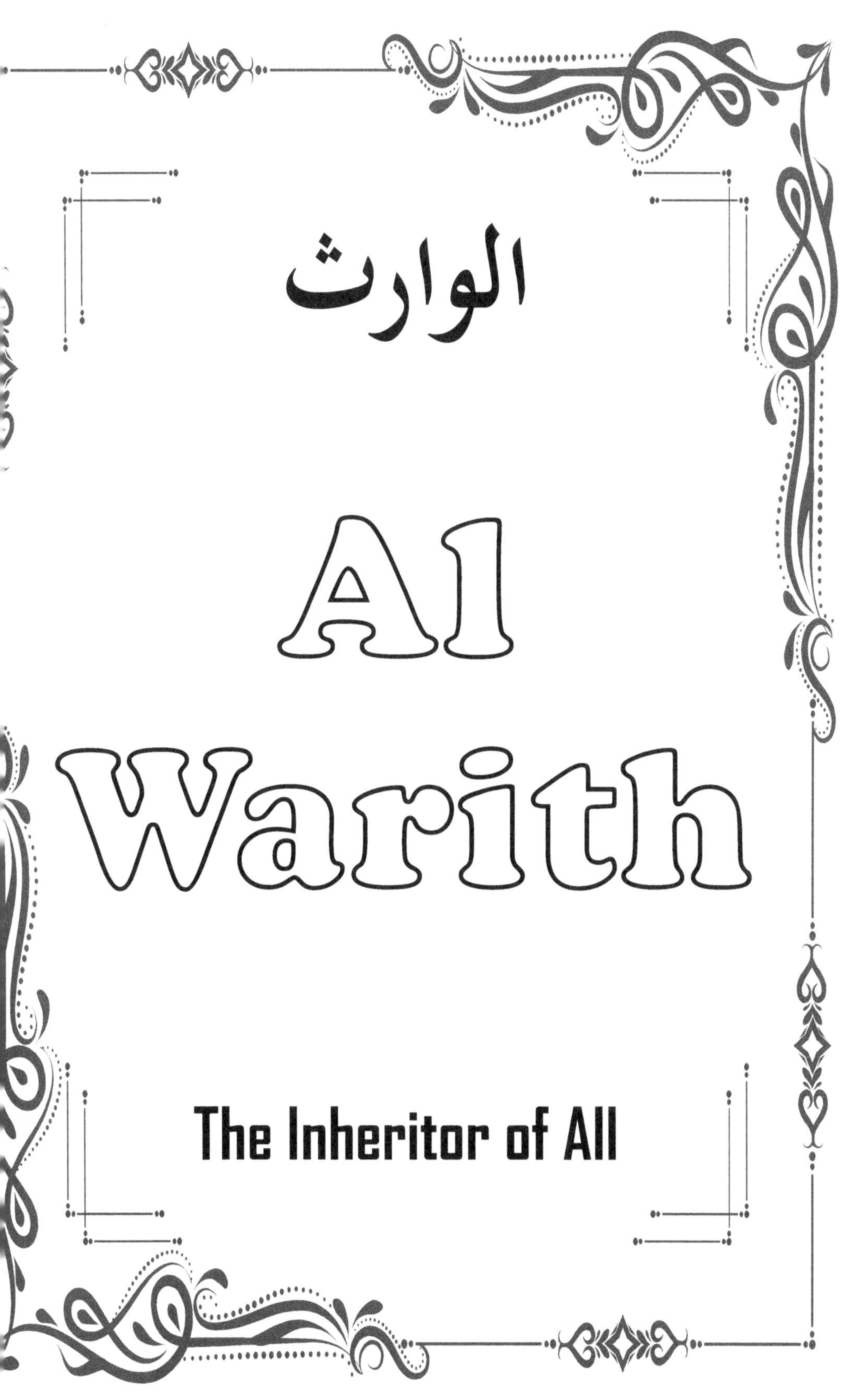

الوارث

Al Warith

The Inheritor of All

الرشيد

Al Rashid

The Righteous Teacher

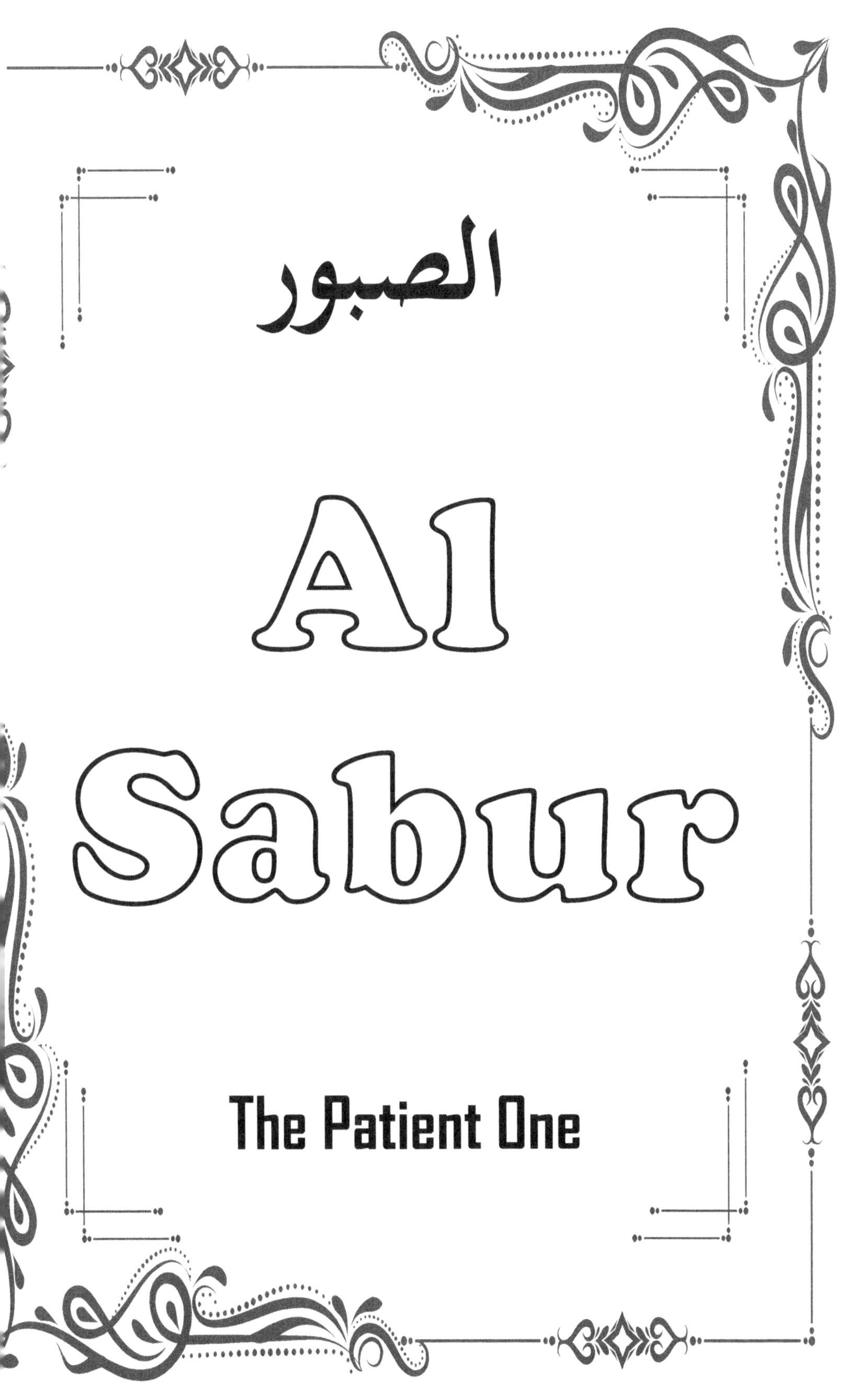

الصبور

Al
Sabur

The Patient One

9 798735 072652